AN APOLOGY
TO THE
IRISH PEOPLE

JOHN M. FEEHAN

Charles Haughey is an outstanding patriot.

> — Sir Geoffrey Howe,
> British Foreign Secretary.

3·80
3·80
4·50
7·00
—————
19·10

GW00676396

RᴄB
ROYAL CARBERY BOOKS

ROYAL CARBERY BOOKS, 121 Shandon Street, Cork.

Trade Distributors:
THE MERCIER PRESS, 4 Bridge Street, Cork.
24 Lower Abbey Street, Dublin 1.

ISBN   0 946645 08 6

BOOKS BY THE SAME AUTHOR

Travel
THE SECRET PLACES OF THE BURREN
THE SECRET PLACES OF DONEGAL
THE WIND THAT ROUND THE FASTNET SWEEPS
THE MAGIC OF THE KERRY COAST
THE MAGIC OF THE SHANNON

Biography
TOMORROW TO BE BRAVE
AN IRISH PUBLISHER AND HIS WORLD
BOBBY SANDS AND THE TRAGEDY OF NORTHERN IRELAND

Politics
THE SHOOTING OF MICHAEL COLLINS
OPERATION BROGUE
THE STATESMAN

Printed by Litho Press Co., Midleton, Co. Cork.

CONTENTS

THIS BOOK IS DEDICATED
TO
THOSE MEMBERS OF FIANNA FÁIL
LOYAL TO THE IDEALS FOR WHICH
THE PARTY WAS FOUNDED.

ACKNOWLEDGEMENTS

The author and publishers would like to thank The Mercier Press Ltd., for permission to quote Bobby Sands' material from the following books: One Day in My Life, Skylark Sing Your Lonely Song, Bobby Sands and the Tragedy of Northern Ireland.

INTRODUCTION

There was once a man with a long-flowing beautiful beard. One day this beard accidentally caught fire and his friends rushed up to him and said: 'Look! Look! Your beard is on fire.'

'I know! I know!' replied the man, 'but can't you see I'm praying for rain.'

ORIENTAL FOLK TALE

This is probably one of the most painful books any author could undertake to write. It is an account of how I placed my trust in the noble words and utterances of an Irish politician, how I believed what he said and how that trust and belief turned out to be naive and misguided. Not only that, but I have reason to believe that through my writings I influenced others to place their trust in him, and indeed to support him at election time. I now feel I have let them down and I have written this book to apologise and ask their forgiveness.

At a time when Charles J. Haughey's standing in the country was at its very lowest, when every hand seemed to have been raised against him, I wrote two books which were regarded by the public as a kind of an antidote to the false and damaging stories being circulated about him. The first of these, *Operation Brogue*, was an account of how the British Secret Service vilified him in a widespread and dirty campaign over a number of years. Sadly they were helped, either wittingly or unwittingly, by many Irish people who should have known better. The British did so because they calculated that he was a serious danger to British interests in Ireland. They believed that Garret Fitzgerald and the leaders of the Coalition would prove sympathetic to those British interests and would see

Ireland's role as coming within the sphere of British influence. On the other hand they thought Haughey was an Irish Republican in the fullest sense of the word, a leader who would put into effect the ideals for which Fianna Fáil was founded and policies which could prove a serious obstacle to the domination of our country by Britain. They saw him, therefore, as their enemy, and when the British identify someone as an enemy they are not too scrupulous as to the means they employ to destroy him.

It is now of some academic consolation to me to realise that the great M16, the powerful arm of the British Secret Service, made the same blunder as I did. They too believed Haughey to be a threat to British interests. They subsequently wasted hundreds of thousands of pounds in a totally unnecessary campaign to destroy a man who was ultimately to prove every bit as sympathetic to British interests as ever Garret Fitzgerald and his Coalition were. 'We did, however, teach him a lesson,' one of them remarked while privately admitting their mistake. 'Haughey must now have a healthy fear of what we can do to him if we want to.'

The second book I wrote was *The Statesman* in which I suggested that Haughey was in the tradition of Pearse, Collins and De Valera and that like De Valera in the 1930s he would stand up to the British, stop spending £500,000,000 per annum copper-fastening the six county statelet, and lead the Irish people towards the ideals upon which the nation was founded.

I was wrong on all counts. He proved to be more in the tradition of John Redmond and the old Irish Parliamentary Party, ready to make obeisance to the British in the hope of getting in return a few unimportant crumbs and a little praise.

Friends and enemies alike warned me: 'Do not trust him,' they said, 'He will use and exploit you; he will use and exploit the national ideal; he will use and exploit anything to get power.'

I could not believe that any leader of the great Fianna Fáil party would make such forceful patriotic statements merely for the purpose of exploiting the people and so I paid no attention to these critics. They also accused him of using the national ideal to get rid of Lynch and to get himself elected as leader of the party, and again of using the national ideal to win votes in the 1987 election and achieve power. When he achieved power, they say, he turned his back on the national ideal and ignored the objectives for which Fianna Fáil were founded. Amid wild cheering he said at a Fianna Fáil Ard Fheis: 'We are not going to be the generation of Fianna Fáil who surrendered to the neo-colonial mentality.'

His critics now accuse him of surrendering to that very neo-colonial mentality he had condemned. Painfully I must admit that on his track record since he came to power these critics were far nearer the mark than I was.

Of course we are all very wise after the event and readers may justifiably ask why did I not spot the trend in time. After all there must have been quite a few red lights flashing. Discerning friends asked me a number of questions: When Colley demanded a veto on the appointment of certain ministers why did Haughey not refuse him head on? I answered that by saying he was trying to maintain unity in the party. It did not occur to me that you do not maintain unity by letting the tail wag the dog.

Why did he give in to Tip O'Neill about the transfer of an Irish diplomat. I replied that he wanted to protect and encourage US investments. Incidentally I have just read Tip O'Neill's autobiography. There is not a single reference in it to either Ireland or Haughey – surely a pointer to O'Neill's priorities!

Why did he not stand up to Thatcher at the time of the hunger-strike? My answer was that it was for the good of Anglo-Irish relations. I conceded, of course, that all these capitulations were mistakes and Haughey had learned from these mistakes and would never repeat them in the future.

Looking back I can now see how I was only inventing excuses and throwing dust in my own eyes. I should have seen that the fault lay much deeper – that he lacked one of the most fundamental qualities of leadership – a quality without which no leader can last – the quality of resolution, the quality of toughness in the face of a strong adversary. Almost every time he came up against a tough situation and an able opponent – especially a British one – he capitulated. On the one occasion he did not back down, the Malvinas/Falklands affair, the telling-off he got seemed to have scared him to such a degree as to cause the magazine *Phoenix* to comment that if now Thatcher sank the *Belgrano* in the Irish Sea Haughey would send her a telegram in support.

There was however one incident in which I was personally involved which should have flashed the strongest warning light of all. The incident happened shortly after the publication of *The Statesman*. The literary editor of the *Irish Independent*, Dick Roche, set up his literary page one Friday evening for publication in Saturday's issue. This literary page contained a number of book reviews including a favourable one of my book *The Statesman*. The following morning the paper appeared and the review had been removed and something else substituted. This was done without Dick Roche's knowledge. I managed to get a proof copy of the page which contained the review before it was removed. I went to Mr Haughey and showed him the page. Here at last was evidence which could suggest that the *Irish Independent* had an editorial bias against him. Haughey now requested a meeting with a director of the *Irish Independent*. I was later told this meeting took place and that Haughey showed the proof page to the director and informed him that if the censored review was not published then he would make the whole thing public.

Nothing happened. The review did not appear and the matter was not made public. The only conclusion I can come to is that the *Irish Independent* stood up to Haughey and he backed down.

This little incident should have warned me, even though it was now too late. If he could not stand up to the *Irish Independent* how could he stand up to people like Thatcher and Reagan? Nevertheless I put the whole thing into the back of my mind. All will be right, I argued, when he becomes Taoiseach.

Well, he became Taoiseach and nothing really changed. A series of incidents in rapid succession forced me to conclude that he had not learned one iota from his past mistakes and that he did not simply have it in him to face the British with firmness and resolution. Instead of the lion hoped for the reality was nearer to a jellyfish with the sting removed. Whenever he faced the British or Americans he made suitable obeisance and caved in.

It now began to dawn on me that his great patriotic speeches were little more than empty rhetoric. I began to cast a more critical eye on the gap between what he *said* and what he *did* and I found that an enormous chasm existed. Speeches and actions were as different as the proverbial chalk and cheese. I now saw with sadness what a fool I had been to believe that he could display the vision and resolution of men like De Valera and Michael Collins in Ireland, Adenauer in Germany and even Thatcher in England. I had got it completely wrong. Not only did I mislead myself but I misled my readers – thousands of them – into believing that Charles Haughey was the leader Ireland was waiting for. I now realise, not too late I hope, my mistake. I also realise sadly, that Ireland would have been far better off had Haughey taken Seán Lemass' advice and kept out of politics. He is far from being the man to weld us into a nation once again.

In order that my readers may fully comprehend the enormous error of judgement I made I find it necessary to sketch in this book the background to the turbulent state of Ireland today; to show how the British establishment operate a criminal regime in the six counties at a level dangerously close to that of the Nazis; how successive Irish governments, including Mr Haughey's, collaborate fully with this criminal regime and are therefore their partners in crime; how the time has now come for thinking people to assess for themselves who, in reality, are the terrorists and who are the freedom lovers.

Many of the truths in this book will be particularly bitter and unpleasant for peace-loving Irish men and women to accept but in most cases I give verifiable facts. Speculation and opinion I have clearly indicated and kept to a very minimum. I have not been swayed by media catchphrases which do not bear up to investigation in depth. I have concerned myself with real politics, the reality of the situation, and not the hype.

Before I began this book I wrote to Mr Haughey. Inter alia I said in my letter:

I am writing in the hope that even at this last moment you will throw out the Extradition Act. I hope you realise that this Act has nothing to do with Extradition. That is already adequately covered. It has to do with showing the nations of the world who is the effective Taoiseach in Ireland – you or Margaret Thatcher. She stood up to you before and won and you lost an election. If she wins this time, you will certainly lose the next election. The whole of nationalist Ireland, which is the ground support for Fianna Fáil, is opposed to this measure and disgusted with what they see to be your weakness.

I wrote two books favourable to you when almost every writer was against you. If this Act goes through I will have to consider writing another book called *An Apology to the Irish People* in which I will publicly apologise to my readers for misleading them.

I do not want to write this book. I would much prefer to write a book in which I could prove that all my predictions were right and that you were the inheritor of the mantle of Pearse, Collins, De Valera. On the national issue however, it is being suggested to me that you will go down in history as the inheritor of the mantle of others not so patriotic.

If on the other hand you steel your soul, reject Thatcher's influence decisively you could go on to win election after election, like De Valera did when he showed no fear of upsetting Anglo-Irish relations.

I do hope therefore that you will throw out this Act. Nobody falls for the idea of Attorney General's consent which is seen as pure whitewash. The Irish public are not fools.

Although Mr Haughey always courteously replied to my letters I got no reply to this one. Surely he could have made some attempt, however feeble, to refute what I said.

I wrote this book without bitterness, without rancour, but with a lot of sadness. The book I really hoped I could write was an entirely different one – one in which I could say and prove from his actions that he was the leader Ireland was waiting for. Indeed I was so sure Haughey would fulfil his promises that I had planned out the chapter headings of that other book. Why I could not write that book is clear now for all to see.

I have no personal quarrel with Charles Haughey. He has always been friendly and courteous towards me and more than once he extended his hospitality to me in his beautiful and tasteful Blasket island home. He is a cultured man with an abiding interest in and understanding of literature, painting and music and we had much in common to talk about. He is also a kind man with a deep feeling for personal human problems, the kind of man who would not hesitate to offer a helping hand to one in trouble.

So while I write with understanding and sympathy I cannot whitewash the harsh truth. He does not possess the capacity for great leadership. He is well down the field. Perhaps I could best describe my position by adapting the words of Brutus: 'Not that I loved Haughey less, but that I loved Ireland more.' And in the end it is Ireland that counts and not the reputation of either of us.

I would like to thank a number of people, especially my lawyers, who helped me by reading the manuscript and the proofs. I shall not mention any of them by name since to do so would only put them in danger of having their homes raided in the next joint British-Irish raids in the south. Here I am reminded of the famous statement of Pastor Martin Niemoeller in relation to the Nazis which I have adapted to suit Irish conditions:

The British-Irish searchers came first for the IRA and I didn't speak out because I was not in the IRA. Then they came for the grass roots of Fianna Fáil and I didn't speak out because I was not in Fianna Fáil. Then they came for the followers of Neil Blaney and I did not speak out because I was not a follower of Blaney. Then they came for those whose names were written in Irish and I did not speak out because my name was not written in Irish. Then they came for the trade unionists and I did not speak out because I was not a trade unionist. Then they came for the socialists and I did not speak out because I was not a socialist. Then they came for me and by that time no one was left to speak out.

I am now speaking out and I hope it is not too late.

J.M.F.
July 1988.

14

ONE

UNION JACK OVER IRELAND

I can verify that the British never told the truth about a single incident in Northern Ireland since 1970.

— FR DENIS FAUL 1982

A good catchphrase can obscure analysis for fifty years.

— WENDEL L. WILKIE

Northern Ireland is part of the United Kingdom — as much as my home constituency of Finchley is.

— MARGARET THATCHER

To understand Haughey's weakness as prime minister one has to take to take a look at that one element, above all others in Irish affairs, which brings out the greatness or debility of an Irish leader. That element I shall call the British Dimension. What is Britain's interest in Ireland? Is it philanthropic and nobleminded? Is it for the good of the Irish people or otherwise and perhaps most important of all, does Haughey know the truthful answer to these questions? Does he grasp what the British are up to?

In order to deal in any effective way with such questions we must recognise and come to close grips with one element which is of great relevance. That element is: *Political thinking in Ireland is ruled to an alarming degree by catchphrases that are virtually without substance.* This woolly thinking is not just confined to politicians but it is also noticeable in the media where one might reasonably expect a more penetrating analysis. (How many times, if ever, has the media dealt seriously with the concept that the British are occupying part of our country in the same way as the Nazis occupied France?)

Scores of these catchphrases, none of which are true, are very prevalent in our media and in political circles. 'The IRA are terrorists', 'The RUC is a decent fair police force', 'Ireland cannot be united by force', 'We must be nice to the Unionists and woo them', 'The British will leave the six counties when a majority wants it', 'There are two nations in Ireland', etc. etc. These catchphrases remind one of the Hitler principle that if you keep repeating lies often enough the people will eventually believe them. The British have reputedly spent millions of pounds floating these catchphrases on the Irish scene and they would now claim they have been highly successful.

These catchphrases, they believe, have now become almost scriptural principles in the Irish media particularly in some television programmes, where real in depth balanced investigation is the exception rather than the rule.

If we look carefully and critically at these catchphrases we notice two things: 1: *they simply do not stand up factually*, and 2: *they work solely for the benefit of British interests in Ireland.* That they do not work in the interests of truth, justice or peace should surely make us suspicious, but despite their savage record in this country one of the last things we ever seem to feel about the British is suspicion. Some of these catchphrases have a special relevance for this book and perhaps if we look at a few of them and strip them down to the naked truth the picture may reveal some unpleasant facts.

One of these catchphrases is: *The British are in the six counties as a peace-keeping force.*

This statement is false. They are quite indifferent to noble concepts like 'peace-keeping' but they do pay lip service to them if they can hope to gain some advantage for themselves. The harsh truth is that the British are in that part of Ireland for strategic and military reasons only. The six counties is an important element in their entire defence system and they have no intention of voluntarily withdrawing whether a majority wants it or not. Not only that but they regard Southern Ireland also as part of that same defence system. This explains why they want to control Southern Ireland, preferably as part of the commonwealth, and if this is not immediately feasible then to have a government in the south subservient to their interests. They would claim that they have had such governments in the south, whether Fianna Fáil or Coalition, since the early 1970s.

On her eastern front Britain has the European countries as her bulwark against Russia but she is wide open from the west. The Russian cruise missiles with nuclear warheads can be launched from submarines out in the Atlantic Ocean and fly in across Ireland and devastate practically all the cities of Britain. Her survival, therefore, could depend on her having along the coasts of Ireland a series of bases from which such missiles could be effectively destroyed in flight.

That is the reason why they still occupy the six counties and platitudes such as 'loyalty to the Unionists' etc. are pure waffle. To understand this clearly and not to be deluded by their propaganda is of the greatest importance – and it is astonishing how many intelligent people are deluded. Their interest is purely self-interest although they have successfully floated the catchphrase that *'they are fed up with the north and want to leave'*. They do not want to leave and will not leave unless forced to do so, and such is their track record that they will not be forced by political action only, even though holding on to the north means that a certain number of British soldiers will be killed. They have calculated statistically what is an acceptable level of deaths and while they remain within that limit they will stay. Nobody seriously suggests that members of the British cabinet will lose much sleep if British soldiers are shot. They are not only interested in the occupied six counties where they are daily tightening their grip but they would also dearly like some kind of military control over the south whereby the British army would have bases and airfields along our coasts. We are not likely to be asked to agree to this as equals but as underlings. Britain does not ask – she demands! And as we shall see she has been most successful with her demands. Britain does not see us as an equal sovereign state with fundamental rights. Rather does she see us as a nation of underlings who have broken away from her and who may be allowed a limited degree of freedom provided we behave ourselves and do not interfere with over-all British strategy. Haughey recently put this point succinctly when he said: 'The historic inability in Britain to comprehend Irish feelings and sensitivities still remains.' What he did not say, however, was: How can the British be blamed for treating us like slaves if we act like slaves? And for our being so he must bear a large share of the responsibility.

At the present moment the British army have at least twenty defence sites against missiles in the six counties. She needs at least as many more in Southern Ireland and she is quite willing to use any means, including violence if necessary, to get them. Those who doubt this might usefully look at her track record since 1969 and pay attention to an extraordinary statement by Humphrey Atkins, former secretary of state for the six counties. He said:

Sixty years ago Britain and Ireland – a lot of Ireland – got separated. I think we can reverse that.

This is a rather strong statement from a top British cabinet minister and the second sentence is of particular interest. Atkins did not say: 'I hope we can reverse that.' He went a lot further. He seemed sure that they could and would reverse the past. Again his assistant Michael Mates said:

It would be important for us, for the two nations, to sing with one voice over defence. The strategic importance of the island cannot be over-estimated.

This is the kind of obtuse arrogance which shows fairly clearly how the British see us.

In the De Valera and Lemass eras such statements would have evoked a sharp public response and rejection by either leader. But there was no such governmental rejection when these statements were made. No one said that there was no question of Ireland reversing the past and becoming again a subservient state. Again no one said that the only way we would reverse the past was by freeing the six counties from the forces of occupation and uniting Ireland once again. That is the kind of language the British understand but there was no one to speak it. We had come a long way down the road of subservience. We were acting out our traditional role of slaves and how could the British be blamed if they accepted our own lowly estimate of ourselves? This silence was a clear sign to them that no leader of the calibre of De Valera would prevent them.

The interesting question here, of course, is: Does Haughey know what is behind British moves? Has he fully grasped what Britain is really up to? There can be little doubt about the answers to these questions.

Speaking to the New Ireland Forum Haughey said:

The British government cannot be allowed to play the role of disinterested peacemaker between warring factions. Britain is in fact, whether she recognises it or not, acting in a partisan role, supporting unconditionally the basic Unionist position by military, political and economic power.

Seemingly exasperated at what seemed to be Garret FitzGerald's inability to see through the British Haughey arraigned him across the floor of the Dáil:

Will you never learn? Will you never understand that no matter what soft words or protestations are used the age-old reality prevails? Britain relentlessly and remorselessly pursues British self-interest no matter whom it hurts or effects.

These were noble words – words that any Irishman could be proud of. In my book, *The Statesman,* I thought those noble words meant something. I was to find out with sadness that they were only words, only meaningless rhetoric, perhaps designed to catch Republican votes. When he came to power on the back of those Republican votes Haughey quickly pushed those words out of his mind. He knows well what the British dimension is but it seems as if he is prepared to take insult after insult and co-operate. Is he trying to capture the Fine Gael-PD yuppie pro-British vote? Only Haughey himself knows the answer, but what is sure is that this gap between his words and his actions, which we will encounter again and again, must raise the most serious questions as to his credibility. If a man is consistently given to U turns how can he be trusted?

Recently we have been subjected to a lot of hype to the effect that Haughey is playing a brilliant diplomatic game. 'On the diplomatic high ground' is the catchphrase being bandied about. I have no evidence whatever that he is playing a brilliant diplomatic game. It seems much more like a political paralysis especially when confronted by Thatcher – like that of the rabbit before the snake. I find it hard to see how ignoring professional killers in a shoot-to-kill policy, allowing Irish citizens to be jailed, harassed and condemned for crimes they did not commit, taking insult after insult without a murmur is 'brilliant diplomacy'. The words 'prudence', 'wisdom', restraint', etc. are also being bandied about daily but unfortunately our media has as yet not investigated the difference between these words and the words 'political cowardice'. To use these words when Ireland is being spat upon and publicly insulted reminds one of the man whose beard is on fire praying for rain. There is no great diplomatic game being played by Haughey. Sadly there is only incompetent capitulation.

A second catchphrase is:*We must do everything in our power to foster Anglo-Irish relations.* On the face of it this seems a reasonable proposition until we examine it a little more closely. If we do we find that 'Fostering Anglo-Irish Relations' is one of the great bluffs, one of the great cop-outs of all time. It is the excuse par-excellence to do nothing. It is regularly on the lips of politicians and pundits of the media, but at the present moment it works one way only.

When the British do something criminal that justifies tough action, we shrug our shoulders and say: 'Ah yes, of course. But we must not do anything to damage Anglo-Irish relations.' And if pressed the Department of Foreign Affairs will tell us, 'we have made our views known'. One of the few growth industries in Ireland is this 'made our views known' industry. We must have a bevy of typists employed 'making our views known' in letters destined for the Whitehall waste paper basket.

Like every civilised nation, we should foster good relationships with other countries, especially our nearest neighbour, but we must do so on the basis that we are a free and dignified people and not a nation of slaves. Unfortunately it is in this latter role we show ourselves to the British.

If we set aside for a moment the political nonsense which is flung at us daily and ask the question: What does 'good Anglo-Irish relations' mean to the British? we will find that it means that which promotes British interests, as Haughey so well put it. This means that the cultivation of good Anglo-Irish relations is an important means of furthering British strategic and military interests in Ireland. 'Good Anglo-Irish relations' to the British is a vehicle whereby they can influence and dominate this country purely in their own interests and at the Irish taxpayers expense. It is a delusion to think that they want to be friends with us. On the contrary, despite their polished coffin-like oratory, there is plenty of evidence to show that they hate and despise us, but they see the advantages of using us through 'good Anglo-Irish relations' and the British are not too squeamish who their bed-fellows are so long as they can exploit and use them.

What does 'good Anglo-Irish relations' mean to the Irish? Unlike the British, the majority of the Irish do not have any real sense of identity as a people, nor do they have any great sense of loyalty to Ireland as a nation. Rather is their thinking dominated by a deep-rooted inferiority complex in the presence of their 'betters' – what Seán MacBride used to refer to as the 'slave mind'. This slave mind is the root cause of much of our troubles. We have always had, and never so much as today, politicians ready and willing to help the British cause in Ireland. They were vociferous at the time of the removal of the oath, the economic war, our neutrality, and many of their successors are still backing Britain. This has the effect of inhibiting them when dealing with the British, whom they see, subconsciously at least, as their masters. This in turn produces a kind of psychological incompetence that makes them wilt away when they come face-to-face with the British.

The British sense this feeling of inferiority and exploit it to the full.

In this situation the Irish unfortunately see 'good Anglo-Irish relations' as a way out, as an escape from confronting reality and dealing ruthlessly with it, as a face-saving device enabling them to genuflect without prostrating themselves completely, as a means of pleasing others.

We probably reached our lowest level of political cowardice in April 1988 when a television programme showed that three Irish citizens were killed in cold blood in Gibraltar seemingly with the approval of the British cabinet. An Irish media comment was as laconic as it was tragic:

Last night the government were not forthcoming with a reaction to the new information which could further harm delicate Anglo-Irish relations.

In other words the British can kill our citizens when and where they like but Haughey will take no effective action except to express verbal concern presumably in case it would damage 'Anglo-Irish relations'! Is it any wonder that the nations of the free world look on us with contempt, and that the British despise us for what we are.

The hard facts are that the track record of British activity in Ireland since 1969 provides the clear evidence as to what their intentions are in the six counties, and what 'Anglo-Irish relations' really means to them. 1969 was the 1916 of the six counties. The Nationalists stopped running and fought. For more than sixty years they suffered from the British regime brutalities similar to those suffered by the Jews from the Nazis.

Senator Edward Kennedy put it succinctly:

The government of Ulster [six counties] rules by bayonet and bloodshed. The struggle today in the ghettos of Derry is for liberty and the right of self-determination, for principles that should be the birthright of all peoples who call themselves free men.

But by 1969 they'd had enough. The Provisional IRA was born. For the first time in the six counties the British were up against a force that would not be cowed and that improved as the years went on to the point in 1988 when the British military conceded that the IRA could not be beaten.

Hopes that all Ireland might become Britain's front line of defence against Russia were seriously dashed. The British did not care a fig for the mouthings of Fianna Fáil, Fine Gael or the SDLP. What these politicians had to say was irrelevant. The British now had on their hands a war with a deadly force that could easily destroy their ambitions. They did not mince words. The Northern Ireland premier Major Chichester-Clarke publicly declared: 'Northern Ireland is at war with the Irish Republican Army Provisionals.'

Reginald Maudling, British secretary of state also publicly declared that the British government was 'now in a state of open war with the IRA.'

The IRA were not seen as criminals, thugs or terrorists – that was to come later.

The British set before themselves one objective and one objective only: *Destroy the IRA.* Social improvements, fair employment, justice in the six counties were irrelevant. To win the war against the IRA was all that mattered and they proceeded to enlist the support of Irish governments led by Lynch, Haughey, Cosgrave, and Fitzgerald. How highly successful this skilled manoeuvre was is there for all to see.

They invented what is now known as 'good Anglo-Irish relations' and in pursuance of this myth they made a series of demands on these Irish governments. As they succeeded bit by bit they could hardly believe how easy it was.

Here are some of the British demands:

1. *Curtailment of Republican Activities in the South.*
This demand was granted. On our statute books we have some of the most repressive legislation in the world. This legislation is aimed mainly at Irishmen and women engaged in anti-British activities who may be convicted simply on the word of a senior police officer without any real evidence. A sample case taken at random is that of Don O'Leary of Cork. He is a young married man with two children. He is a member of the Irish Society for the Prevention of Cruelty to Children and also a member of the National Association of Tenants. He

was instrumental in setting up Gaelscoil Peig Sayers, an all-Irish speaking school. He is a member of Sinn Féin which is a legitimate registered political party. On 18 May 1987 his home was raided by police and some election posters were taken. After six months delay he was arrested and charged with IRA membership. The charge was based on the possession of these posters. What does not seem to have been taken into consideration was that several thousand of these posters were freely available for many years as election literature, and if possession was an offence, then some thousands of Cork citizens should also have been charged. O'Leary gave sworn testimony that he was not a member of the IRA. Yet he was sentenced to five years for membership of the IRA – the proof offered being that he possessed the posters. He is now serving his sentence in Portlaoise jail.

This in effect means that anyone at all, and this includes you or I, could be sent to jail on the flimsiest of evidence.

This legislation has helped to fill our jails with innocent young men and women whose sole offence is that they reject British occupation of our country. The British are of course delighted with our performance.

We also yielded to their demands for the suppression of Nationalist comment by introducing the now notorious Section 31 of the Broadcasting Act which prohibits interviews on radio and television with members of Sinn Féin even though they are elected by the people: that means one MP and over ninety councillors. These representatives of the people may not be interviewed on RTE, yet members of the British terrorist SAS unit, the RUC, and the Castlereagh torturers, the Loughall and Gibraltar killers have full access to our airways.

One of the worst elements of Section 31 is the fact that any organisations banned under the British Emergency Powers Act are *automatically* prohibited from RTE. This means that if the British decide to ban anyone in any country in the world that person is automatically banned by RTE. This effectively gives the British government power to decide what is suitable for the Irish people to see and hear on RTE. Have we similar power over BBC? You may be quite sure we don't even have a say.

It has also had another bad effect, best expressed in the words of the International Federation of Journalists, the umbrella group for all National Unions of Journalists, who lumped Ireland with other oppressive regimes such as Turkey, South Africa and countries behind the Iron Curtain:

We agree completely .... the most dangerous effect of the present Section 31 is the creation of a general climate in which restrictions on the media and free journalism are accepted and defended. In such a climate it becomes far too easy to introduce new restrictions to 'solve' political problems by shutting up people instead of addressing the real problems.

This was a tremendous victory for the British. It has the effect of slanting most stories on Northern Ireland towards a pro-British bias and in this way contributes greatly to the overall strategy of the British to make the Irish people think like they do.

Recently a New York newspaper accused RTE of putting pressure on journalists not to interview people of a Republican viewpoint, even if they were not members of a proscribed organisation. The same paper also stated that the playing of Nationalist songs was strongly discouraged. When have we last heard 'Kevin Barry', 'The Boys of Kilmichael' or 'The Boys of the County Cork' played on RTE? Can one imagine the BBC discouraging 'Roll out the Barrell' or 'It's a Long Way to Tipperary'?

According to this legislation De Valera himself, who because he advocated the use of violence in the north would now, if he were alive, be banned from RTE. So also would Collins, Pearse, Connolly and all the other great leaders, while at the same time officers and members of the Black-and-Tans would have full access to our airways. Has any country in the world ever debased itself so much?

Haughey spoke out against this legislation and publicly expressed the view that Sinn Féin candidates should have access to radio and television. More important still the Fianna Fáil Ard Fheis of 1987 passed a resolution demanding that all elected representatives be given full freedom of expression on the air. Perhaps Haughey had his eye on Sinn Féin No. 2 votes! Whatever his motive, he genuflected again to the

British and renewed this odious piece of legislation after he was elected. How pleased with him Thatcher must have been! Why did he so debase himself? Only he can answer that question and so far he has remained silent. Yet there is one element worth looking at. Could it be possible that the Sinn Féin case is so overwhelmingly unanswerable that the politicians are afraid to engage in debate with Sinn Féin? Gerry Adams challenged Peter Barry to a public debate. Barry refused. Recently Danny Morrison challenged Haughey to a public debate and Haughey refused. What are they afraid of? Could it be that Section 31 is not really aimed at protecting the public but is aimed at protecting Irish politicians from having to publicly defend their pro-British policies? One way or another the British won hands down. But what a sad day for Ireland that the word of its Taoiseach cannot be trusted.

2. *Access by the British Secret Service to Irish Intelligence.*
This demand was fully acceded to. The British now have access to Irish police computers. This means they have available to them all the information the gardaí have on every citizen. A recent article in a Belfast Sunday newspaper says:

As part of a cross-border exchange plan RUC men are collecting intelligence in the south at a special office inside garda headquarters in Dublin .... A six-strong team of police from Dublin are believed to be on permanent liaison duties with the RUC although the number of them based at known RUC headquarters is not known. At least three detectives from Dept 3 of E Branch, the official name of the Special Branch, are based in an office of the first floor of the new building in Dublin's Phoenix Park.

Can one imagine the West German government giving such facilities to the KGB and East German secret police?
A further extension of this ignominious capitulation is a unique invention know as *The Prevention of Terrorism Act*. This has nothing to do with the prevention of terrorism. It should have been called the *Extortion of Information Act*. Its purpose is to collect information only. Irish citizens can be arrested on arrival in Britain and kept for seven days without charge. A

process known as disorientation is often used in interrogating them. First of all the gardaí usually supply the British with every detail known on the individual, who is astounded at what the British know about him. She or he does not know that her/his own local garda station may have given the information. Then the disorientation starts: breakfast and dinner are given within an hour of each other, and then nothing for the rest of the day. The next day no breakfast is given but dinner is. Sleep is also disoriented – the prisoner being awakened every hour or every two hours, or at irregular intervals. The result is that the prisoner is confused, suffering and prepared to say almost anything to get out. If he or she refuses to give the information the British want then they can charge the prisoner and she or he can be sentenced to five years imprisonment. Thousands of our citizens are being subjected to this treatment every year, even some members of the Fianna Fáil party, yet we still keep giving full co-operation and information. If the British police perpetrate some major piece of brutality on a detainee, as happens from time to time, all we do is give the usual 'we have made our views known' letter, or another cliche – 'we are monitoring the situation'. The British by now realise that these letters are meaningless and that we know they are meaningless. If we had any respect for ourselves as a nation we would surely stop providing the British police with information and would perhaps introduce legislation to monitor the scores of M16 agents who come and go in this country without hindrance. Again the British triumphed.

3. *The right of British Security Forces to cross the Border.*
This demand was granted. British helicopters land almost weekly in the Republic, search houses and take off again without hindrance. In one short period there were nineteen such incursions and, as if to show the utter contempt the British have for us, Tom King stated publicly in the House of Commons: 'None (of the nineteen) resulted in a formal apology by the ambassador in Dublin or a statement of apology by myself.' British killer squads have come into the Republic and abducted Irish citizens and in some cases killed them on Irish soil, but we took no effective action.

Haughey has been made fully aware of the extent of garda co-operation with these killers. He has been given details of who the people concerned are – yet they are still there. Here a question may be asked: What is the real reason the Stalker Report was not made public or shown to the government? Is it because it would reveal the extent to which the British have infiltrated the gardaí without hindrance?

Two questions asked in the Dáil elicited the information that over a period of years there were 1, 300 incursions into the south. These were the ones known to the government. How many more are unknown?

To set this in its proper context one must ask the question: Would Norway, Finland, West Germany or Austria allow the KGB to cross their frontier and harass their citizens when they liked? Would Britain? Tom King has again given the answer: 'We could not accept any deliberate incursion into Northern Ireland by the Republic's security forces.' Once again we have been put in our place by our 'betters'. They can come and go as they please into our territory but dare we cross the border into our own territory occupied by them.

These are only three out of scores of demands which we so foolishly granted. There must be others of which we know nothing and which will come to light in the distant future when the state papers become public. One of those, of which I have no definite information, concerns an alleged instruction issued by the Coalition government to our embassies not to engage in or to support any Nationalist propaganda that would embarrass the British.

It is when we look at these capitulations in the light of the opposite scenario – those requests made by the Irish government to the British, all of which have been *rejected and refused* – that we have good reason to be ashamed.

Our request that, like the case of Hong Kong, a statement of intent by the British to leave ultimately was *rejected*.

Our request during the hunger-strikes to make concessions was *rejected*.

Our request to stop gerrymandering constituencies was *rejected*.

Our request to transfer Republican prisoners in Britain to Northern Ireland on humanitarian grounds so that their relatives could visit them was *rejected*.

Our request to remove the ban on flying the Tricolour in the six counties was *rejected*.

Our request to cease blocking the border roads was *rejected*.

Our request to cease using plastic bullets which are prohibited in Britain but not in the six counties was *rejected*.

Our request to close Sellafield which is damaging the health of thousands of our citizens was *rejected*.

Our request for the Stalker-Sampson report was *rejected*.

Our request to exercise clemency towards the Birmingham Six and the Guildford Four was *rejected*.

Our request to reform the courts in the six counties was *rejected*.

Our request to cease killing unarmed civilians was *rejected*. (British security forces have killed upwards of 130 unarmed civilians including old women and children and only one member of these forces was charged. He was convicted and sentenced to life imprisonment. Yet he was released after three years and rejoined his regiment).

Here we have the harsh reality that we yielded to *every* demand made by the British and in return they *rejected* every demand we made on them. I am concerned here with facts not with conjectures or with hype. Who can now doubt that things like 'good Anglo-Irish relations' are only British devices to get their way with us?

With the exception of negotiations conducted by De Valera and Seán MacBride the British have walked rings around us on every occasion. It is as though in our negotiations with Britain we have given full expression to an extraordinary incompetence, to our slave mind, to our forelock lifting and, if you pardon the crudity, to our arse-licking. In my book *The Statesman* I suggested that Haughey was the leader to pursue the policies of De Valera and MacBride and get the Irish up off their knees again. Events proved my forecasts sadly wrong. Haughey has unfortunately shown himself to be every bit as accommodating to the British as Lynch, Fitzgerald or Spring. The Irish are still being trampled upon and Haughey has remained inactive. All those brave hopes I had written about turned out to be only so much dross. Looking back now in the light of all that has since happened I can hardly believe how gullible I was.

This brings me to another catchphrase based completely upon a falsehood: *Violence will not achieve a united Ireland.*

It is really hard to understand how so many otherwise intelligent Irishmen give off that piece of nonsense, without taking a closer look at it. It is like saying 'We want good crops but we do not want any frost', 'My beard is on fire but I am praying for rain'.

Every civilised human being abhors violence in the same way as he abhors death on the roads, cancer, storms, accidents etc. but in dealing with the British violence is a fact of life. A catchphrase like that simply flies in the face of the track record – the known facts about Britain.

In each of the thirty odd countries that won their freedom from the British, violence was the deciding factor. The people of these countries, like the people of the six counties, tried constitutional means, they tried negotiations, they tried appealing to world opinion, they tried all peaceful means open to them, and everything failed. Then they resorted to violence and succeeded. On the other hand Scotland is a very good example of a country that abandoned violence and what happened? She was completely integrated with England. Had she held out, like Ireland and so many others, she would most likely be a free land today.

Michael Collins realised that fully when he said:

While England explains the futility of force by others it is the only argument she listens to.

De Valera made it quite clear to the American ambassador that if he had an army large enough he would not hesitate to invade the six counties. He expressed his philosophy on violence quite clearly:

I never said and I am not going to say now that force is not a legitimate weapon ..... I know that in history it is seldom that foreign tyrants have ever yielded to any other .... It is a long wait they destine themselves to who rely on tyrants suffering a change of heart.

This statement of De Valera's is an acute embarrassment to the leadership of Fianna Fáil today. If De Valera made that statement now he would most likely come under the provisions of the Offences Against the State Act and perhaps be charged on the word of a police officer and sent to jail.

That great Irishman George Russell (AE) who abhorred force and who opposed the 1916 Rising realised this:

Although I have always condemned violence we got nothing in Ireland by peaceful means. Yes, all the freedom the Irish have attained has been by fighting, violence and bloodshed.

Even Margaret Thatcher agrees with that point of view. She said:

You have to be prepared to defend the things in which you believe and be prepared to use force to secure the future of liberty and self-determination.

For sixty years the Nationalists of the north tried constitutional means to get some movement on their plight and they met with nothing but contempt. It was only after a long and bloody struggle by the IRA that the British gave any concessions. Such small crumbs as they have got came from violence and not constitutional means. The same happened in all the thirty odd countries occupied by Britain.

Why then do so many people fall for this non-violence catchphrase?

First of all the British have spent millions in promoting the 'non-violence' propaganda. It is not because they are against violence as such but because they realise that the IRA only are their enemies, that IRA violence could bring about unity and that the IRA must at all costs be crushed. The British do not care a fig about the SDLP whom they regard as harmless ineffective orators who will never bring any real change. Their contempt for the ill-advised Forum is one clear indication that violence is the only language they understand. However regrettable, these are hard, cold, provable facts.

It is a centuries old British maxim to get the Irish to do their dirty work for them and they have succeeded admirably in getting Irish governments to suppress the IRA, to jail people like Don O'Leary and indeed to spend £500,000,000 of the Irish taxpayers' money in doing so solely for Britain's benefit.

What is particularly regrettable about all this scenario is that most of the media have swallowed these catchphrases hook, line and sinker. They have accepted the British line without any indepth investigation or analysis of Britain's real motives. As well, many of them have spent far too much energy in silly personal abuse of Haughey instead of concentrating on Britain's real motives and of Haughey's failure to stand up to them.

I too, in my own way, have failed and that is why I am writing this apology. I cannot however be accused of taking Britain at her face value, but I did something equally unwise – I took Haughey at his face value. I portrayed him as a man most likely to put a stop to the British domination and exploitation of our country. Instead he has allowed the British to tighten their grip on the six counties, to tighten their grip on the Republic and bring it more securely into her net. This is hardly what Fianna Fáil was founded for and it is very unlikely that the grass roots support this policy.

If in the past I believed and trusted Mr Haughey too readily, I hope that I shall not be guilty of such foolishness again. For this reason I am a little concerned at a number of strange straws in the wind which I am afraid have not been sufficiently investigated by most political writers – straws which could indicate that some preliminary steps are being taken to bring the whole of Ireland further into the grip of the British and that Haughey may well row along.

After a meeting with Thatcher, Mr Haughey and Mr Lenihan made great play of a phrase 'the totality of relationship'. At the time that seemed to refer to the north and to some movement on partition. But could it have another meaning? Could it mean the return of the Republic to the Commonwealth? When dealing with politicians like Mr Haughey or Mr Lenihan, for whom principle is not necessarily the guiding star, one should examine every statement from all

angles. For example Haughey said that the Irish people are
not prepared to see neutrality 'eroded'. What does he mean by
'eroded'? Why did he not use the words 'destroyed' or 'ended'?
Again in Dáil Éireann he said that when a satisfactory
political solution on Northern Ireland was arrived at the most
appropriate defence arrangements for the island as a whole
would be gone into. He did not define 'satisfactory political
solution'. Does this mean a united Ireland? Does it mean
power-sharing? Or does it mean merely a statement of intent to
withdraw at some vague future date by the British?
Unfortunately Mr Haughey has not told us and commonsense
therefore suggests that we treat everything he says with the
utmost caution, that we study his words carefully and above all
that we pay the most careful attention to what he does not say.

In this clouded atmosphere it would surely be only wise and
prudent for the Irish people to suspect something in the air –
something about which we are to be kept in the dark until our
psychological condition is such that we will accept it meekly
like the sheep the politicians believe us to be.

These are but leaves in the air, yet leaves in the air are
fairly good signs of what way the wind is blowing. We should
not concentrate our gaze on the impressive and beautiful trees
only, but we should take a prudent look at the concealed roots.
If the Irish media could allow such matters engage their
attention instead of whispering about Haughey's private life
they could be doing the country a very great service.

But the real thrust of Britain's effort to absorb us has been in
their approach to the Nationalist paramilitaries. As I have
already said, the first and major task the British have set
themselves is the complete destruction of the IRA, the INLA
and other such forces. This task has now priority over
everything else. British military thinking sees no hope for a
domination of Ireland as long as these paramilitaries continue
to remain active and to enjoy substantial support from the
civilian population. In pursuit of this policy the British see
murder, blackmail, torture, deprivation and terror as
legitimate weapons. Their pursuit of victory through violence,
however, would have little hope of success if the Nationalist

paramilitaries could slip across the border and lie up in the safety of the south. So the task of winning over the southern government to the British point of view was tackled with intelligence, vigour and devilish cunning. Ireland under De Valera or Lemass would not have fallen for their ploys but luck was on their side in that they were dealing with feeble politicians like Lynch, Cosgrave, FitzGerald and now Haughey.

The British operation was crowned with phenomenal success. Within the space of a few years they had the Irish government following the British line in a most subservient way, committing the entire resources of the Republic, the army, the police, the foreign service, the radio and television and even the legislature to maintaining the Orange statelet and copper-fastening the border in full co-operation with Her Majesty's forces. And what particularly delighted the British was that the Irish taxpayer was paying for all this to the tune of £500,000,000 per year – a sum which could build thousands of houses yearly for homeless young married couples as well as making a significant dent in our massive unemployment figures.

One British politician said to me:

Think of what we have achieved. Ten years ago you burned down our embassy in Dublin and most of your population hated us. Now we have you eating out of our hands and your government doing our bidding.

My mistake of course, in all of this, was to believe that Haughey saw through the British and that he would, like De Valera, at once put a stop to their machinations. He saw through them all right, but not being of the same calibre as De Valera, he did not have the guts to stand up to them. So he should not be too surprised if history records him as the man who brought blighting shame not only on the Fianna Fáil party but on the Irish people as well.

The British dimension in Ireland means this: British interests come first.   Murder, torture, brutality are legitimate weapons.   Those who resist them are 'terrorists', and the Irish taxpayer pays £500,000,000 per year to help finance this and our politicians and media carefully nurse 'good Anglo-Irish relations'. Over and above all it is now clear that the British dimension in Ireland has been one of victory beyond their wildest dreams. It is to my shame that I believed Haughey was the leader the Irish nation was waiting for and that I foolishly tried to convince the Irish people that such was the case. I now have to swallow my words and painfully agree that many of the critics were right and I was wrong. I hope my apology has not come too late. And I hope it will inspire those members of Fianna Fáil who still believe in the ideals of its founders not to allow this once great party to become the hind tit of the British, and not allow our people to become informers for the inheritors of the mantle of the Black-and-Tans.

TWO

ON OUR KNEES

The annals of all nations bear witness that an enslaved people always suffer more deeply from those of its own blood who take service under the conquerors than it suffers under the conquerors themselves.
— EDWARD A. FREEMAN

The silence of the people is the lesson of kings. She (Queen Victoria) is the official head and symbol of an empire that is robbing the South African Republic of their liberty as it robbed Ireland of theirs. Whoever stands by the roadway cheering for Queen Victoria cheers for that empire, dishonours Ireland and condones crime.
— W. B. YEATS ON THE VISIT OF QUEEN VICTORIA

The Irish are pigs.
— HER ROYAL HIGHNESS PRINCESS MARGARET

... wouldn't you rather admit to being a pig than being Irish.
— SIR JOHN JUNOR IN *THE SUNDAY EXPRESS*

The British dimension in Ireland has not changed since the battle of Kinsale, the massacre at Drogheda, the famine of 1846 and the Black-and-Tans of 1920-21. It is still the same pursuit of self-interest which rejects all morality that does not advance British interests, which deems any act, including mass murder, as only good or bad in so far as it promotes her objectives. Her long and bloody history in this country has resulted in the slaughter of between 30,000,000 and 50,000,000 Irish men, women and children – and she has not changed one iota. Lecky wrote in the last century that the war in Ireland as conducted by the British was a war of extermination. The slaughter of Irishmen was looked upon literally as the slaughter of wild beasts. This killing is ongoing through Bloody Sunday to Loughall, to Gibraltar. Why then do our politicians grovel and fawn and trust her so much?

The answer to that question raises two important elements:

1. The extraordinary slave mind of the Irish and
2. The probability that our politicians do not want a united Ireland.

There has been, as yet, no adequate study of that extraordinary element in Irish life known as the Slave Mind. This is quite surprising as it is the greatest single fungus growing on Irish society today. It is a fungus which has choked, trottled and impeded every movement on the road to national advancement.   The late Seán MacBride, Nobel Peace Prizewinner, had this to say:

Every country that has been the subject of foreign domination or colonialism inevitably suffers from some degree of slave mentality. This does not affect the fundamental desire of the Irish people to achieve a united and free Ireland; it does however, at times make them ambivalent in their attitude. As has been pointed out by C.S. Andrews this ambivalence or acceptance of the status quo is more noticeable among our present day ruling classes and academics, than among the ordinary people of the country whose national outlook and traditions are sound ... Many of our own politicians, academics and media people have become subservient to this 'slave mentality'.....

Just as agressive colonialism in Ireland by Britain has bred a 'slave mentality' among a large section of our people, the feeling that Britain has a God-given right to interfere in our affairs is deeply ingrained in the minds of those who populate the inner recesses of the British establishment.

One of the North's most enlightened priests, Fr Des Wilson, comments:

The English government is strong in Ireland because the Irish are weak ... every time our masters have called on us to condemn each other, many of us have obeyed. Yes, your honour, colonel, sir, what Irishman do you want me to condemn .... just show him to me, your honour, and I'll condemn him. I only wish, your honour, colonel, sir, that I had a forelock to touch, but if I get down on my knees, sir, will that do .... I will still do whatever it is you require of me, because I know that you are superior to me in every way ... You are English and I am Irish, your honour ....

For hundreds of years we have been crawling at their feet and begging a few crumbs from their table. They were the masters and we were the hewers of wood and the drawers of water. Perhaps the most extraordinary expression of that servility was contained in the words of Daniel O'Connell's son John, when he spoke in glowing terms of some Irish peasants who starved to death rather than fail to pay the rent to the landlords. 'I thank God,' he said, 'I live among a people who would rather die of hunger than defraud the landlords of their rent.'

Have things changed much since then? Could an Irish politician of today say: 'I thank God I live among 250,000 unemployed people who would rather stay unemployed than deprive the British of the £500,000,000 a year it costs us to keep the country divided?'

Ingrained attitudes like that do not simply change overnight and even today large numbers of the Irish live out that servile role in their daily lives. They have come to love their degrading servitude and they remain on their knees, still grovelling before their masters, still wearing the invisible chains of slavery. For them the capital of Ireland is London and they pay extraordinary homage to any person with the drop of blue blood, no matter how stupid or thick that person may be. Most of their ideas, when they have any, are taken from England and their lives are heavily influenced by formulae driven into their heads by incursions of British television and British newspapers. These attitudes seem to have produced such a deep lack of confidence in themselves and their country that they must perforce turn to England for moral support, for opinions and advice, even though there are far more competent Irish men and women available. 'You have the phenomenon in this country that some of our civil servants and army officers are more English than the English themselves,' said Lieutenant-General M.J. Costello in an *Irish Times* interview with Seán Cronin. 'Their view of NATO is from London ..... Since the foundation of the state the Irish

bureaucracy has believed that whatever was British was best
... They ape and adopt British ideas.'

Large numbers, unfortunately, of our politicians suffer from
this slave mind, this inferiority complex and they are never
happier than when they are grovelling before the British and
promoting the British ethos in Ireland. They are part and
parcel of that millieu which General Costello so despised.

This extraordinary attitude has made the job of the British
so much easier that it prompts one very embarrassing question.
Do Irish governments, Fianna Fáil or Fine Gael, want a united
Ireland?

This question is at the very core of Anglo-Irish relations but
how often, if ever, do we find it dealt with by the media?

*I have to say that I have no solid concrete evidence to show
that any of the main southern political parties really want a
united Ireland under a single government in Dublin.* I use the
words 'solid' and 'concrete' specifically to distinguish between
something real and practical and not something contained in a
speech. In any view of a united Ireland one must clearly
distinguish between the verbosity of politicians and the actual
reality of what they are prepared to do in practice – and as far
as a united Ireland is concerned it must be obvious to everyone
that they are not prepared to do anything effective.

I once put the above question to a prominent Fianna Fáil
politician a man well versed in *realpolitik* and his answer was
quite revealing:

'Suppose we had a thirty-two county republic,' he said,
'What do you think Dáil Éireann would be like? With the
north in we would have an extra seventy seats of which at least
fifty could be held by Unionists. Can you not imagine what
chaos that would cause? Fianna Fáil would never again be able
to get an over-all majority. It would be the end of party
dominance, and I may tell you the end of a lot of jobs and
Mercedes for the boys. The Unionists would permanently hold
the balance of power; indeed we might very easily have a
Unionist Taoiseach in a Coalition. No matter how much we
care about the plight of the Nationalists in the north, we do
not care all that much. No. What we want in the north is some

kind of peace so that we won't be troubled by them – they're a bloody nuisance. Oh no, a united Ireland would be a disaster for us. But,' he added with a grin, 'if the Unionists had any sense that's what they'd be looking for.'

Few statements sum up the attitudes of various Irish governments as well as that and I would be hard-put to find any evidence proving that statement wrong. Of course I can find plenty of speeches, particularly at Ard Fheiseanna, the Garden of Remembrance, Bodenstown, etc, which say the opposite but speeches no longer impress me. I trusted them too much in the past and I am now convinced only by effective action. We have had sixty-seven years of freedom and if we were really serious about partition we could have it solved long ago. But the harsh truth is most Irish politicians, despite their speeches, simply don't want a united Ireland. They don't want to lose their power, their perks and their massive pensions. I find it extremely painful to have to say this but it is the truth.

There are others also who seem to think on similar lines. Former secretary of state Humphrey Atkins said in a BBC interview: 'It is my belief that if we were to say to the government of the Republic: All right, we will leave Northern Ireland, you can have it, they would turn and run. They don't want it.'

I have no evidence whatever to show that Atkins was wrong. The evidence I have unfortunately points in a different direction. Irish politicians seem to be interested primarily in votes and many of them are prepared to be Republicans, Unionists, Conservatives, Maoists or anything you like if it leads to an increase in votes.

Of course the escutcheon of the Unionists is not without blemish. One should not pay too much attention to the 'sense of identity' of these same Unionists. Their 'sense of identity' can be best measured in terms of hard cash. Their 'Britishness' gave them 90% of all the 'goodies', the jobs, the housing in the six counties.

They want to hold on to that immensely lucrative position and their 'Britishness' is the best way of holding on to their privileges. If they could get back to their degree of domination they would become Nationalists or Marxists or anything else that would enable them to hold on to this power. One should, therefore, take with the proverbial grain of salt the woolly thinking of some media pundits about their 'sense of identity', 'Britishness' etc. The Unionist position is governed more by hard cash and power than by any sense of identity. One writer put it: 'Their loyalty is to the half-crown and not the crown.'

A clear-headed and penetrating look at Irish politics reveals the harsh but tragic facts:
1. The British do not want a united Ireland for strategic reasons.
2. The Unionists do not want a united Ireland because they would lose their privileges.
3. The Irish do not want a united Ireland because a united Ireland would seriously delimit the power of the political parties and drastically curtail their emoluments, perks and jobs for the boys.

Upton Sinclair shrewdly remarked: 'It is difficult to get a man to understand something when his salary depends on his not understanding it.' In the midst of this cynical power play however are two thousand graves and over two thousand heartbroken families in Northern Ireland.

Only Sinn Féin and the IRA it seems really want a united Ireland and they are prepared to suffer torture, brutality and even death to achieve it. How many of the present cabinet would be prepared to do a stint in Long Kesh concentration camp for their country? My readers will have to answer for themselves the questions: Who are the inheritors of Tone, Pearse, Connolly and Clarke? Who best puts into practice the ideals which Fianna Fáil was founded to achieve?

With these gloomy disagreeable truths as a back drop we get a hint as to why we trust the British so much, why we have debased ourselves so much, a debasement which must be unparalleled in world history. Indeed it would take an entire book to record our long track record of fawning and cringeing. Here, however, I can only deal with a few recent political happenings where in the eyes of the world we must have reached rock bottom in servility and in which both the British and Irish dimensions stand out in sickening clarity.

1. The Forum

Our constitution is clear on our national territory – it is the 32 counties of Ireland. Since the inception of the state we have made this known worldwide. Why then was it necessary to call a convention and waste £1,000,000 of the taxpayer's money in telling the world what it already knew? Can one imagine the West Germans calling together a Forum to define the status of East Germany?

The explanation for this nonsense may be found in the rise of a kind of political yuppism which tried to supplant truth and fact by new ideas which sounded more avant-garde and bizarre and which gave a certain kudos to second or third class historians and politicians.

The pioneer of the Forum was Garret FitzGerald, our prime minister at the time; a political windbag who had already made himself a laughing stock in Europe by his hopping kangaroo-like from country to country while his own country rushed ahead towards bankruptcy. His handlers tried to sell him as a new inspired visionary bringing Ireland into Europe. In reality he was little more than a well-meaning political blunderer. But then it seems as if one can sell anything to the Irish. How Barnum would have flourished here?

The real reason, of course, for the Forum was to break Sinn Féin and the IRA in the six counties and politically promote the SDLP. (Isn't it interesting that the British, the Unionists and the Irish politicians have been so united in their fear of Sinn Féin?)

The British, of course, supported the concept of the Forum because anything that could damage Sinn Féin would have their full support, especially as the Irish taxpayer was footing the bill. They had not however the slightest interest in the outcome, since as far as they were concerned there would be no change whatever in the six counties that would even slightly interfere with British strategic interests. The Forum would be another red herring, another delay postponing the moment of decision. So they looked on and laughed at the Irish making fools of themselves.

The Forum report, so far removed from the ideals of the founders of the state, was humbly offered with due respect and obeisance to the British who rejected it out of hand and poured contempt on its contents. It is doubtful if Thatcher even read it. Any intelligent teenager in the six counties could have told the Forum that the British are an army of occupation who want military bases and all Summits, Forums and Crusades will not alter that fact one iota.

At the 1984 Forum-Summit Thatcher treated FitzGerald like dirt, rubbed his nose in the gutter, and in so doing humiliated the whole Irish nation. Those of us who hoped that he would stand up to the British in the same way as De Valera, Seán Lemass or John A. Costello were sadly disappointed. Like an errant schoolboy he took his caning and returned meekly to the dunce's corner of the political classroom, and commenced work on something else even more servile.

The British correctly assessed that FitzGerald would come crawling back for more and that they could negotiate a new agreement with him which would be far more advantageous to their interests than anything in the Forum. This judgement proved to be faultless. FitzGerald did come back, and began the process of negotiating what came to be known as the Anglo-Irish Agreement. The Forum and the £1,000,000 of the Irish taxpayer's money was forgotten. The chancelleries of Europe must have seen us as first-rate political idiots.

2. The Anglo-Irish Agreement

The British entered the negotiations with the purpose of achieving four objectives:

1. A clear cut declaration by the Irish government that despite the Constitution, they accepted the six counties as part of Britain in such a manner that the Irish government could never claim internationally that the six counties were Irish or conduct any campaigns to have a united Ireland.

2. A complete and total commitment by the Irish government to crush the IRA so that the six counties would remain securely British.

3. That the Irish taxpayer should pay for all this.

4. To give nothing of consequence to the Irish in exchange.

They were completely successful in all four objectives and had these objectives embodied in the Anglo-Irish Agreement registered with the United Nations.

The British secretary of state was delighted. In Brussels he gleefully stated:

We have signed an agreement in which the prime minister of Ireland, notwithstanding the fact that he faces and has to live with a Constitution which has aspirations of sovereignty over Northern Ireland, has in fact accepted that for all practical purposes and *into perpetuity there will not be a united Ireland* (Italics mine).

And Mrs Thatcher said:

Far from representing any threat to the union of Northern Ireland with the United Kingdom the agreement re-inforces the union ..... This is the first time that the legitimacy of the Unionist position has been formally acknowledged in a formal international agreement.

The proclamation of 1916 was in tatters and Britain once more fooled us, as she had done so often in the past.

FitzGerald and his handlers projected a massive whitewash job in which most of the Irish media co-operated – how tragic that most of our media fell for the banal! Carefully orchestrated messages of congratulations came from various other countries. In the Dáil FitzGerald read out a list of government leaders who sent congratulatory messages on the Agreement. What he did not read out, of course, were those countries that did *not* send messages of congratulations. In his book *Fooled Again?* Anthony Coughlan states:

A glance at the list shows important omissions. One doesn't suppose the Taoiseach missed Russia or China very much, though they are rather important states. But what about India? No Norway. No Sweden. No Austria. No Finland. No Iceland. Not a single South American country. Not a single African country. No New Zealand ... But the Irish media were so impressed by the people who sent messages that they paid no attention to the many who did not.

Is it more than a coincidence that those countries which approved were members of NATO? Were they welcoming another potential NATO member? Another nation the flower of whose manhood could be expected to die so that Britain might survive?

But in the midst of all this degradation and disgrace there was one voice that spoke for Ireland – the voice of Charles Haughey leader of Fianna Fáil. His key points were:

The Agreement seeks to bolster up the political structure of Northern Ireland when that structure is the root cause of the problem ... It represents an abandonment of Irish unity and a copper-fastening of the partition of our country. It will not bring peace or stability but only serve to prolong violence and strife ... The Agreement is in total conflict with the Constitution, and in particular Articles 2 and 3 ... For the first time ever the legitimacy of the Unionist position which is contrary to unification, has been recognised by an Irish government in an international agreement ... The Agreement will lead the Irish government into an impossible political situation in which they will find themselves assuming responsibility for actions and being involved in situations, particularly in the security field, over which they will have no control ... The British guarantee to the Unionists has been re-inforced by the Irish government, and the government has also endorsed the British military and political presence in Ireland ... What is proposed is that the Irish government, by becoming involved in the existing British administration in Northern Ireland, however tenuously, will afford that administration an acceptance, an endorsement and an approval, which constitutionally they cannot and should not do ... The Inter-Governmental Conference only formalises an existing right of the Irish to make its views known, but in return we have given everything away ... The impression is conveyed to our friends around the world that we are now fully satisfied about the situation in Northern Ireland, that they need no longer be concerned about us and that we have finally accepted the British presence in Ireland as valid and legitimate ... It is a triumph for British diplomacy which undermines the very basis of Constitutional Nationalism ... Treaties are binding in international law but there is a well-established exception to the general rule if what was done was manifestly contrary to a state's internal law of fundamental importance ... In the Irish case there could hardly be a more manifest violation of that law than an international agreement which accepted the right of the British government to exercise sovereignty over the north of Ireland ... Since neither the government of the day nor the Oireachtas has any authority to act in conflict with Articles 2 and 3, no future Irish government need, unless it so wishes, be bound by the provisions of any international agreement which are incompatible with those of the Constitution ... We will certainly not be prepared to accept it in its present form.

This was a speech worthy of the very best in Fianna Fáil –

worthy of De Valera or Pearse. It stated clearly the position of all Irish Nationalists, the position enshrined in our Constitution, the position for which so many brave Irishmen and women gave their lives.

Apart from his condemnation of the disgraceful abrogation of the Constitution Haughey, in this speech, brought out two points of major importance which our media missed:

1. A clear objection to any security co-operation between the Republic and the discredited security forces in the north.

2. A clear indication that a future Fianna Fáil government would not feel itself bound by any part of the agreement which seemed to them to infringe the Constitution, and a clear hint that it would not accept as binding any such parts of the Agreement. He even sent Brian Lenihan to America to canvass support of the American government against the Agreement.

I remember reading this speech with a sense of joy bordering on euphoria. At last we had a leader of courage and resolution who would stand up for the Irish people. At the time I was putting the finishing touches to my book *The Statesman* and I felt fully justified in all the predictions I had made in that book on the greatness of Haughey.

What a pity I did not delay its publication a little longer. If I had done so I would never have published it and I would most likely have consigned the manuscript to the dust-bin where it really belonged.

Haughey's condemnation of the Agreement won widespread acclaim for him among traditional Fianna Fáil supporters as well as among the majority of people within the country. This support eventually put him back into office again as Taoiseach and the country looked forward to a leader of courage and resolution who would stand up to the British and not delimit his country's heritage.

One of his first acts after becoming Taoiseach was to visit the United States and here we looked forward to a pronouncement from him that would slam the Agreement and that would once more reiterate Ireland's Constitutional position not only for the benefit of the forty million Americans of Irish descent, but for the world at large.

Unlike FitzGerald and his advisers, who were such political blunderers that they thought the American government were their friends, Haughey had taken the measure of these politicians. They were Americans first and foremost and that meant they they supported the British in the north for strategic reasons. They were Irish on St Patrick's Day and at Irish Embassy dinners and ballad sessions – but it stopped there. They fully supported the British occupation of the north. That was made quite clear to all and sundry when President Reagan visited Ireland as part of his electioneering campaign. His secretary of state George Shultz speaking at the Stockholm disarmament conference said:

The United States does not recognise the legitimacy of the artifically imposed division of Europe ... the attempt to impose divisions on Europe is inevitably a source of instability and tension ...

The artificial division of Ireland seems to have slipped Shultz's memory. But Haughey did not let him forget it when he said:

Would it not be one of those noble and generous acts which have happened from time to time in American history and the final tribute to the enormous contribution the ancestors of forty million Irish-Americans have made in the building of America and to the valuable part they have played and still play in the political life of that democracy, if the President, in addressing both houses of the Irish parliament in June, were to declare the United States does not recognise 'the legitimacy of the artificially imposed division' of Ireland either and that henceforth the United States will include the re-establishment of the historic unity of Ireland as a major objective of her foreign policy.

Reagan ignored Haughey. The partition of Ireland was vital to American strategic interests. It is only if such divisions worked against American interests did the noble sentiments of Schultz apply.

Ireland looked forward to Haughey's speech in Washington rejecting the terms of the Agreement as he had done in Dáil Éireann and once again publicly calling on Reagan not to recognise the division of Ireland. Many hoped that it would be the kind of answer made by De Valera to Churchill after the war – a speech which shot him to the highest point of popularity ever reached by an Irish statesman.

Instead Haughey's speech dashed the hopes of his supporters and made every Irishman hang his head in shame. It was a fawning speech in which he reversed his earlier speech in the Dáil, a speech which grovelled before the Americans and British. Amidst the splendour of the White House, the dinners and the flattery, he now made it clear to the world that he accepted the Agreement and would work it to the full. By this he turned his back on everything he had previously said. By this he now accepted Britain's right over Northern Ireland, Britain's partition of the country, and promised full co-operation with the internationally discredited security forces of the north in maintaining the border and the partition of our country. Brian Lenihan's visit to America now took on the role of a burlesque act, like Sancho Panza on a jack-ass tilting at windmills. How could any American politician now treat Haughey with respect? Or indeed how could any Irishman?

He had let down the ideals of the Fianna Fáil party who stood by him; he had let down the Irish people who elected him; but above all he had let himself down by throwing his credibility into doubt and by raising the question as to whether any trust whatever could be placed in his word.

All that had been said to me again and again after the publication of *The Statesman* by people who bore Haughey no ill-will, but whose perception was, it seems, much sharper than mine. 'He cannot be trusted,' they said. 'Political principle, integrity and honour are not high priorities with him. He will one day belie every thing you said about him if he thinks it suits his immediate purpose. He will most surely let you down.' But I did not believe them. I still trusted him.

But that Washington speech proved to me how wrong I was. Reagan and the British stood up to him and he didn't have the guts to fight back. My critics were right and I was wrong.

Stalin used to say that in going forward if you meet steel: stop; if you meet mush: continue. In coming up against Haughey the British met mush – and they continued – continued on to get more and more concessions from him, more

and more abrogations of the rights of the Irish people. They
had taken his measure as a weakling just as Thatcher had at
the time of the hunger-strike, and won, and now they were
winning all the way.

When De Valera founded Fianna Fáil he referred to those in
power as '... *under contract with the enemy to maintain his
overlordship.*' He founded Fianna Fáil specifically to destroy
that 'contract' and that 'overlordship'.

And now the great Republican Party of Fianna Fáil, under
the leadership of Charles Haughey, are as much 'under
contract with the enemy' as ever the old Cumann na nGaedheal
– Fine Gael were. Pearse and the men and women of 1916, De
Valera and the founders of Fianna Fáil must have turned in
their graves. Their dreams were now in ruins.

3. The Extradition Act

One of the most important concessions the British won as a
result of that disgraceful Agreement was the Extradition Act.
There were adequate extradition provisions in existence as
between any two democratic countries but this did not suit the
British. They had to present their case before the Irish courts
and this was very often embarrassing to them. What they
really wanted was an automatic extradition, without having to
go before a court, so that they could extradite whoever they
liked, bring them to the six counties and torture them until they
got 'confessions' and then try them in one of their questionable
courts. This concession the Fine Gael Coalition gave them
through the minister for justice, Mr Alan Dukes. Under pressure
Mr Dukes agreed to a safeguard, *viz*, that the *British* attorney-
general would have to approve of the extradition. This was
described by a leading senior counsel as 'putting the fox in
charge of the hen house.' This was so appalling that it left
even Fine Gael supporters speechless and showed the terrible
depths to which Fine Gael had sunk in their subservience since
the days of John A. Costello who said in reference to
extradition:

In order to prevent any further controversy or discussion on this point ...
there can be no question of our handing over either to the British or six

counties authorities persons whom they may accuse of armed activities in Britain or the six counties.

When Haughey introduced his own Extradition Act in 1964 he said:

What I am saying does not apply to offences of a political, revenue or purely military character for which warrants of arrest may be received. These warrants will not of course be enforced.

But when this new Fine Gael Act was being introduced he excelled himself in his condemnation of it. He spoke with the voice and sentiments of Pearse, De Valera, Collins and all the great Irishmen who went before him. He spoke words that made every Irishman and woman in all parts of the world proud of him. This was the Haughey I had written about in *The Statesman.*

The bill, although passed by Fine Gael and Labour, did not become law for a year and in the meantime Fianna Fáil came to power and Haughey was Taoiseach. Now everyone, including Fianna Fáil, believed he would put this disgraceful bill aside. But it was not to be. Once again his noble words proved to be only so much trash. He capitulated completely to the British and brought the act into force with one minor futile amendment. That amendment was the substitution of the Irish attorney-general for the British attorney-general, which of course meant that young Irishmen had no access to the courts and only the good-will of the attorney-general stood between them and torture and a show trial. This was no safeguard, but something had to be done to hoodwink the grass roots of Fianna Fáil.

One may ask the questions: 'Why should there be so much fuss about extradition?' Is there not extradition between all democratic countries? On the surface that seems a reasonable question until we ask: Would West Germany extradite its citizens to East Germany? Would Egypt extradite its citizens to Israel? Would Spain extradite its citizens to Gibraltar? The answer is in all cases an emphatic no! No self-respecting country would extradite its citizens to a regime occupying by force part of its national territory – that is of course excepting Ireland. It is to our eternal shame that we are the only country in the world prepared to extradite our citizens for political offences.

What is even worse we know that in extraditing our citizens to Britain or the six counties we are extraditing them to a regime where they have virtually no chance of a fair trial and where they may be subject to the same kinds of beatings and torture for which the British were found guilty by the European Court.

The track record which includes the Maguire family, the Guildford Four, the Birmingham Six shows beyond all doubt that in practice there is no such thing as British justice. What purports to be British justice is in most cases subject to British political expediency. Indeed Lord Denning, once Britain's leading judge, publicly stated that it is preferable that some innocent men remain in jail rather than the British system of justice be impugned. How Hitler and Stalin would have delighted in that opinion!

One little item however which seems to me to be of considerable importance was largely ignored by the media who regretfully seem to emphasise shadow rather than substance. It was what Mrs Thatcher said:

I indicated to Mr Haughey how deeply I felt about the changes in extradition that have been made (i.e. role of Irish attorney-general). But he indicated very firmly to me that if the arrangements are not satisfactory they will be reviewed because he wants to make the arrangements satisfactory ... He is as anxious that people should be brought to justice as I am and he did give me considerable reassurance on that point.

There are a number of questions arising out of this statement which the media did not ask.
1. Mrs Thatcher felt reassured by Haughey. What does that mean? To be 'reassured' Mrs Thatcher would want only what Fine Gael gave her – complete and absolute right to extradite whom she liked. Did Haughey 'reassure' her of that and that the introduction of the attorney-general was only a gimmick to throw dust in the eyes of his own backbenchers? He 'assured' her that if the arrangements did not work satisfactorily he would review them. Does this mean that if Mrs Thatcher

cannot extradite whom she likes Haughey will change the act? Only such action as that would be 'satisfactory' to Mrs Thatcher. Did he tell the Fianna Fáil party of his assurances? 2. She says that Haughey was anxious to bring people to justice. What kind of justice? The justice given to the Birmingham Six or the Guildford Four, or the Maguires or the Diplock Courts? Is that the kind of justice Haughey wishes to give the Irish people? Did he also tell this to the party? Unfortunately the Irish media did not examine any of this in depth.

In consequence of all this, the terrible question which faces the Irish people is: What can one believe from Haughey? What credibility has he left? If in the near future he were to come out one hundred per cent on the side of Nationalism, Republicanism and a United Ireland, who would believe him?

In *The Statesman*, I wrote:

Today ... to revive our country and shake off the British yoke requires the sure steady hand of a statesman of the highest calibre ... He (Haughey) has the ability. He has the political acumen. He does not grovel before the British.

How wrong I was. How terribly wrong. And I am now wondering if, even in this book, I can purge my stupidity.

THREE

THE CRIMINAL STATES

It is clear that large areas of the security system and the administration of justice in Northern Ireland are corrupt. In that they mirror the state of Northern Ireland itself ...... many people are gravely concerned that no action of our government should be seen to condone the abuses of the northern judicial or security system.

— CHARLES J. HAUGHEY

You know when we were in Ballymurphy .... we had these people really fed up with us, really terrified. I understand what refugees must feel like in Vietnam...... after every shooting incident we would order fifteen hundred houses searched – fifteen hundred!

— BRITISH LIEUTENANT IN SIX COUNTIES

Although you moan about Ireland at least you're going to have a chance to shoot some bastard through the head .... You're there to kill people and to see guys killed.

— BRITISH PARATROOPER IN SIX COUNTIES

At this point we might usefully take a look at the extraordinary composition of the six county statelet – the statelet to which Mr Haughey gives full co-operation and to which he extradites our citizens and calmly ask ourselves is it a democracy or a criminal state? If we opt for the latter and if it is a criminal state then the logical consequences are that we in the south are dangerously close to the criminal ethos because of our support.

The six county state had its origins in the seventeenth century when, after the defeat of the native Irish chieftains, the British occupation forces evicted hundreds of thousands of

Irish Catholics from their lands and homes and replaced them with English and Scottish Protestants and Presbyterians. The present Unionists in the north are the descendants of these settlers. Those of the dispossessed Irish who remained at home and did not emigrate became the hewers of wood and drawers of water, menial servants in their own country, subservient to their dispossessors in the way the Jews in occupied countries became subservient to the Nazis. The present Nationalists are descended from these dispossessed Irish.

The French Revolution spread ideas of freedom and equality which were highly odious in the eyes of these settlers, particularly as some of their own class were affected by them, and so they banded themselves, with the approval of the British government, into an extreme sectarian organisation known as the Orange Order to ensure absolute and uncompromising dominance over their confiscated territory. This organisation might be described as the Klu-Klux-Klan of Ireland and was, through intimidation, imprisonment and bloodshed, to dominate all aspects of life in the six counties down to the present day.

Because of its discipline, its tightness, its offer of security, the Orange Order succeeded in stripping its members of all individuality and substituting therefor the mind and philosophy of its leaders. It became a vast political machine involving thousands of minions who had a personal interest in seeing that all decisions concerning jobs, housing, welfare, education and public affairs in general conformed to the over-all designs and plans of its bosses. Its great weapon was hatred. With consummate skill it succeeded in inculcating into its members a fanatical, venomous, inflammable hatred of everything and everyone Irish. Mainly by this weapon it created in the six counties a statelet where virtually all who did not support the Orange Order were dehumanised. With extraordinary callousness Britain, mother of democracies, supported and financed this artificial state.

The British government of course had its own reasons for giving its full support to the Orange Order. They were only putting into effect their old formula 'divide and conquer'. A divided and disunited Ireland posed little threat to Britain and could be kept in line and subjected easily if it were really necessary. British Chief Secretary Sir Robert Peel put it in a nutshell: 'I hope they may always be disunited. The great art is to keep them so.'

In 1921 when Britain sued for peace in the war between the IRA and the British army, Ireland was given a measure of freedom roughly corresponding to the kind of dominion status enjoyed by Canada and Australia. But this independence excluded an undefined area in northern Ireland where the Unionists, as the adherents of the Orange Order called themselves, had a majority. Michael Collins had agreed privately with Lloyd George that this area would not exceed three, or at the very most, four of the Ulster counties. This was later confirmed by both Churchill and Lloyd George to Tim Healy MP. Collins was satisfied that the small Northern statelet of three or four counties only, would become an unviable economic unit and would eventually unite with the rest of the country. Practically alone among the Irish political leaders of the time Collins was the one with a real effective concern for the Nationalists of the north. 'No matter what happens,' he told them publicly, 'no matter what the future may bring, we shall not desert you.' He never went back on that promise. When things got bad in the north he sent large consignments of arms and ammunition to help the Nationalists, and when the brutality of Sir Henry Wilson, the Unionists' military adviser, resulted in the killing of scores of Nationalists Collins had him shot. The Fine Gael party today, who claim Collins as one of their heroes, are somewhat embarrassed by his actions on the north, particularly since under present legislation he could be extradited to the north.

Later when Collins was killed under most mysterious circumstances his successors in the new Free State government of the south, seemingly anxious to be good members of the British Commonwealth, abandoned Collins' republicanism and handed over six counties instead of three. It is interesting to note here that the original idea of the Orange Order was to take over all nine counties of Ulster. However, when they did their sums, they found that the Nationalist majority in all *nine* counties of Ulster would be too great to manipulate, so they chose only *six* counties which would prove much easier to gerrymander and dominate. The inclusion of the three other counties, Donegal, Cavan and Monaghan, would in the words of Sir James Craig, first premier of the six counties, 'Reduce our majority to such a level that no sane man could carry on parliament with it.' This must be the only case in the history of the world where a new state refused extra rich prosperous territory which could be had for the asking. It was in this unusual but calculated way the state of Northern Ireland, based entirely on a privileged class, came into being.

When some of our yuppie historians today speak of a Unionist majority they forget to say that it is an arranged and contrived majority. It is not a democratic majority. There are areas in Wales and Scotland where the population do not want to be part of Britain so if majority rules why are they not allowed to secede? Sadly such fundamental questions are rarely, if ever, examined by our media.

A favourite catchphrase among lightweight politicians is that you cannot 'bomb' 800,000 Unionists into the south. If that is so how come you can 'bomb' 600,000 Nationalists into the north?

Around 45% of the population of this new statelet were Nationalists who did not want to have any hand, act or part of it but they were forced against their will, on the one hand by the British and on the other by the new Irish government in the south. This is a most important factor in the understanding of the present war in the north, and of why the Nationalists have resorted to force. The Nationalist population of the six counties want to join up with and be part of the southern Republic but successive southern governments have cold-shouldered them in such a way as to make them feel unwanted. This sad point crops up again and again. *Oratory apart, there is no evidence whatever to show that either of the main political parties in the south want an independent united Ireland.* This unfortunately is *realpolitik*. In the allotment of blame for the present violence in the six counties successive southern governments must surely bear a heavy burden of responsibility which speechmaking cannot easily conceal.

In the new six county realm the Orange Order set about

consolidating their position by creating what was virtually a police state. Their first step was to gerrymander the constituency boundaries to ensure the almost total disenfranchisement of the Nationalist minority. The population of the six counties was approximately 55% Unionist and 45% Nationalist so that on this basis out of eighty-two local councils the Nationalists should have controlled about thirty and the Unionists fifty. But so well was the job of gerrymandering accomplished by Sir John Leech KC that the Unionists controlled eighty councils and the Nationalists only two. The Unionist chief whip, Major L. E. Curran made no bones about it: 'The best way to prevent the overthrow of the government by people who had no stake in the country and had not the welfare of the people of Ulster at heart was to disenfranchise them.' There was uproar from the few opposition deputies at this statement. The Unionists now realised that Curran had gone too far and they had this statement discreetly removed from Hansard, the official parliamentary reports, when it was being printed. Whatever official did this piece of 'censorship' bungled the job by deleting Curran's statement and leaving in all the attacks made on him by the opposition!

This kind of disenfranchisement continued throughout the six counties leaving the Nationalist population with no voice whatever in the running of the state. County Fermanagh was a particularly interesting case. Mr E.C. Ferguson, Unionist MP for Enniskillen said: 'The Nationalist majority in County Fermanagh, notwithstanding a reduction of 336 in this year, stands at 3,604. I would ask the meeting to authorise their executive to take whatever steps, however drastic, to liquidate this Nationalist majority.' Apparently the necessary steps were taken. Even though the Nationalists have a 51% population majority here they were only able to get seventeen seats on the council as against the Unionists' thirty-six.

The devilish job of gerrymandering gave them virtually complete control over all state and semi-state employment. They used this predominance to the maximum and with great success. Of all government jobs 90% were filled by Unionists. Those few jobs that went to the Nationalists were usually menial clerkships. Now and again a moderately important job would be given to a non-Unionist so that if any adverse comment came, say from America, they were able to point to this appointment as camouflage. One cabinet minister, however, Sir Dawson Bates, had such a hatred of Nationalists that he made it clear to his senior civil servants that not even the most junior clerk in his ministry was to be employed if he were a Nationalist. In one purge Sir Basil Brooke, later Lord Brookeborough, sacked one hundred and twenty-five employees when he found out they were Catholics. His exact words were: 'If we in Ulster allow Roman Catholics to work on our farms we are traitors to Ulster.' When he publicly urged all employers not to give work to Catholics there was an outcry, but the prime minister, Lord Craigavon, backed him up fully. 'There is not one of my colleagues who does not entirely agree with him,' he said, 'and I would not ask him to withdraw one word.'

Since virtually all private industry was in the hands of members of the Orange Order the same pattern applied. There were very few jobs for Nationalists. One employer said publicly that in fifty years his firm had only one Nationalist employee, and that was a case of mistaken identity. In the great shipyard of Harland and Wolff out of ten thousand workers there were only about three hundred Nationalists, and they were given only the lowest paid and most menial jobs. Again in the county of Fermanagh, where there was a Nationalist majority, only three of the seventy-four school busmen employed by the Education Committee were Nationalists.

Another important step in the control of Northern Ireland by the Unionists was the formation of the police force. But first they passed the Civil Authorities (Special Powers) Act 1922. This Act gave the police amazing powers of search, arrest, detention, imprisonment without trial, suspension of inquests, prohibition of meetings, burning of publications, confiscation of property, flogging of prisoners. In this Act Regulation 22B says that a person shall not be excused for not answering any question on the ground that the answer many incriminate him. It was of that act that John Vorster, prime minister of South Africa, said he would willingly swap all his anti-Communist powers for this one law. This appalling act was later replaced and strengthened by the Northern Ireland Emergency Provisions Act 1973, consolidated in 1978 and was described by a British Civil Liberties commission as 'contrary to the fundamental principles of democratic government.' But it still remains in force and as I write these lines it is being daily put into effect, with the full approval of the British government, *and the co-operation of the Fianna Fáil government.*

This police force is almost entirely Unionist, and since its formation it has operated with a brutal efficiency which can again only be compared to that of the Gestapo or the South African secret police. Torture and even murder have been its most common weapons. Night after night these armed police raided Nationalist houses, dragged men and women and children out of their beds, kicked and beat them up, smashed furniture, pictures and family heirlooms. And there was no redress. The highly respected *Manchester Guardian* said:

The Unionists have an important ally. They have a coercive police force of their own .... They have become the instruments of religious tyranny .... parading their districts at night with arms, harassing, threatening, beating and occasionally killing their Catholic neighbours and burning their homes.

The following terrible statistics speak for themselves. In 1971 there were 17,292 raids on Nationalists' homes. In 1972 this had risen to 36,614 and in 1974 had risen again to 71,914. *This is approximately two hundred houses raided per day.* This police conduct resembles the conduct of the Gestapo towards the Jews in occupied countries. But even worse these raiders now have the full co-operation of the Irish police who assist them by providing information – and all this under a government led by Charles Haughey.

Perhaps more rotten still were the auxiliary police force known as the 'B Specials'. They were an exclusively Unionist sectarian force who were allowed to keep arms and weapons in their homes and who actually participated in ruthless and gruesome pogroms against Nationalists. In the dark of the night, aided by Unionist paramilitaries, they attacked Nationalists areas, burned houses, indeed sometimes whole streets, evicted the old, the poor, the sick, women and children and rendered them completely homeless. It is estimated that 60,000 people were thus driven from their homes, and in Milltown Cemetery alone there are close on 1,000 graves of men, women and children killed during these pogroms.

Well might the respected *Manchester Guardian* again comment:

Whilst envenomed politicians in the Ulster parliament are voting themselves power to use torture and capital punishment against citizens whom they forbid to defend themselves while they scarcely attempt to protect them from massacre, some of their own partisans in Belfast carry wholesale murder to refinements of barbarity hardly surpassed in Armenia and Constantinople.

Today very little has changed. Anyone caring to check this out should spend a few days strolling around the Nationalist areas in Belfast. There they will see real brutality in action. The British army has now entered upon the scene: Saracens firing shots into Nationalist areas: houses searched where furniture is broken and smashed 'To teach these fucking Irish a lesson'; spot checks where people, including pregnant women, are put up against a street wall, searched and beaten with rifle butts. There is hardly anyone living in a Nationalist area that has not experienced this brutal harassment. But one can travel freely through the Unionist areas without seeing a British soldier. Regrettably the British army have a long string of killings to their credit, and the few who ever appear in court are usually found not guilty. The admitted figure of killings of *innocent* people by the security forces is 136. This figure *does not* include killings of Nationalists or other paramilitaries – just ordinary, innocent men, women and children. In the beginning the Nationalists treated the British army with courtesy and often gave them cups of tea in the street. But they learned their bitter lesson and this has long since ceased. Indeed Northern justice must have reached its most outlandish point when a young Nationalist was sentenced to *six months imprisonment* for writing NO TEA FOR DAD'S ARMY on the gable-end of his house.

As late as June 1988 the GAA in Armagh were forced to

protest publicly at the conduct of the British soldiers towards their players, four of whom have been told that they would be shot dead. In June 1988 a number of 'under-10' children were playing a match when members of the British army entered the field, interrupted the match and called the young players 'little Fenian bastards'. One wonders has Mr Haughey any sympathy for these 'little Fenian bastards'? If he has then his collaboration with the British army is very hard to understand.

Worse still was in store for the Nationalist population when the Special Air Service, more generally known as the SAS, came. Whether one likes it or not these specially trained men are the real terrorists. They wear civilian clothes, travel in plain cars, carry knives, daggers, sub-machine guns and the outlawed pump-action shotguns. They are also issued with a special glove, steel-lined and mailed so that it can tear a man's face to pieces. One of its special functions according to the *British Army Land Operations Manual* is to set up special 'assassination parties'. The type of individual which can be found in this force may be judged from the methods used when they stormed the Iranian embassy in London. Having felled one man with the butt of a rifle they then shot him twenty-five times. They put twelve bullets into another man and twenty bullets into yet another. Commenting on this operation Margaret Thatcher said it made her 'proud to be British'. She was probably proud to be British too when they killed the Irish in Gibraltar.

In the North they operate mostly along the border and especially in south Armagh. Their object is (1) to kill on sight and without trial suspected IRA people, and (2) to terrorise the Nationalist population by torture, blackmail and at times even murder. In one month thirty young civilians were shot at from passing cars by the SAS. So bad were their activities that the Civil Rights Association had to publish a booklet called *What to Do if the SAS Shoot at You*. One of the more chilling parts reads:

Provided you are alive when the shooting stops, pretend to be dead until the squad moves away, otherwise they might try to finish the job. If there is any army post nearby do not worry. It will not be manned or if it is the occupants will be busy writing a press statement to say that no military personnel were involved in the shooting.

One of the most frightening books ever written on Northern Ireland has been written by two priests, Fathers Denis Faul and Raymond Murray entitled *SAS Terrorism – The Assassin's Glove.* This is a history of the atrocities committed by this unit in the six counties backed up by signed, witnessed statements, photographs and maps. Reading it makes one almost lose faith in human nature. Yet under Fianna Fáil the Irish security forces are passing information to these hoodlums and helping them terrorise the Nationalists of the north.

One member of the SAS told journalists in Dublin that his job was to cause explosions and bombings in Northern Ireland so that the IRA would be blamed. Seemingly he spoke out of turn. Shortly afterwards he was shot dead by his erstwhile colleagues.

One cannot also rule out the possibility that there is a certain amount of experimentation being carried out by the British army in the six counties. This is the first campaign in a developed society which is a part of what is supposed to be a democracy. New techniques, new methods and new weapons are being tried out. All these, or some of the more successful, may be used later in riot-control in Britain itself. In this sense the military lessons to be learned in the north might well be seen to be worth the cost in lives and money. The callousness of such a policy is by no means outside the orbit of the British ruling classes.

I think I could not be accused of exaggerating if I suggest there is much more than a doubt hanging over the activities of the British army in the six counties. And if the forces of law and order do not administer justice and are themselves guilty of criminal acts then one can begin to understand how young men and women are forced to resort to violence.

Torture of Nationalist suspects is the accepted norm and is carried out with the knowledge and approval of the British government. This was clearly shown when that government was convicted at the Court of Human Rights in Strasbourg.

Many of the officials responsible for the torture were subsequently promoted instead of being punished and later the Queen of England graciously conferred honours on some of them. One can imagine the outcry in the media if the President of Ireland even received a Sinn Féin supporter! But when the Queen bestowed her honours most of the Irish media made obeisance in silence.

The methods of torture used in the six counties by both the British army and the police were based on techniques successfully used by the Gestapo, the KGB and the South African police, and perfected by the British in Cyprus, Aden and Kenya. In the terrible Hola prison in Kenya prisoners who were not even charged were made to work scraping dry earth with their bare hands in temperatures of 120F while their British army guards lashed and beat them. The excuse given by the then English secretary of state for defence was: 'Experience has shown, time after time, that unless hard-core detainees can be got to start working their rehabilitation is impossible!' This prompted Mr Sidney Silverman MP to intervene and ask, 'Who told the Right Hon. Member that? Stalin?'

The methods used in the six counties were mainly:

1. Making a man stand in what is known as the 'search' position, i.e. single finger only of each hand touching the wall, legs apart and far back resting on the toes with knees bent, for long periods. This was a speciality of the Nazis and Russians and was known as the 'Stoika'.

2. Kicking the legs from under a man in the search position so that he falls and batters his head on the ground.

3. Heavy beating with batons on the kidneys and testicles in the search position.

4. Kicking the testicles while in the search position. For some reason this is quite popular with the police.

5. Stretching a man over benches with two powerful electric fires under him thus burning his privates and then kicking him from underneath in the stomach.

6. Banging a man's head against a wall, beating it with a rubber baton for long periods.

7. Squeezing the testicles with a large pincers. The police say that the excruciating pain of this will make a man sign almost

anything.

8. The use of electric instruments, such as a cattle prod.

9. Inserting iron instruments up the anus and bursting it.

10. Finger searching the anus and then sticking the unwashed finger in the prisoner's mouth.

11. Tying the prisoner flat on the ground and several police urinating on him.

12. The psychological torture includes Russian roulette with a revolver, beating men in the darkness, threats against a prisoner's parents, spouse and children and the use of amphetamine drugs.

These appalling methods are fully documented by hundreds of signed statements and while they shock all right-thinking people the British government and the police see them in a different light.

Hundreds of statements from prisoners have been published confirming this torture and there has scarcely been a book written on Northern Ireland which has not dealt with it in one way or another. Gerry Fitt MP said in the House of Commons: 'When the true story emerges of what has been happening in the interrogation centres the people of the United Kingdom will receive it with shocked horror and resentment.' One wonders what Mr Haughey would say if one of his children were subject to such torture? Yet he is quite willing to extradite other people's children to be brutalised in this way.

In Castlereagh Interrogation Centre a staff of trained interrogators were given the task of getting confessions of guilt out of prisoners and on the basis of these confessions it was an easy matter to obtain convictions in a Unionist court even though the prisoners denied the confessions. In a terrifying and disturbing book *The Castlereagh File* Fathers Denis Faul and Raymond Murray itemised hundreds of cases of the most excruciating torture carried out at Castlereagh. Worst of all perhaps was the fact that the men responsible for this torture knew that not only would their careers not suffer as a result but their prospects were likely to be enhanced.

The interrogators start by trying to break the prisoners' resistance by psychological disorientation. He is put into

solitary confinement in a cell where highly sophisticated
electronic equipment controls the level of noise, lighting and
temperature. He is usually left without food for twenty-four
hours. Then he is given a large meal and then a second large
meal an hour later so as to distort his sense of timing and
thereby upset his mental balance. Then the real works begin.

We are fortunate in having a detailed written account from
Bobby Sands of how he was interrogated here. As well as that
we have a magnificent long poem which he wrote dealing with
this monstrous subject:

> I scratched my name and not for fame
> Upon the whitened wall;
> 'Bobby Sands was here,' I wrote with fear
> In awful shaky scrawl.
> I wrote it low where eyes don't go
> 'Twas but to testify,
> That I was sane and not to blame
> Should here I come to die.

He was put into a cell to await his turn, without his shoes:

> The floor was cold on stocking sole
> And boots forbidden things,
> For one might die if one might tie
> A noose with lacing strings.
> For tortured men seek death's quick end
> And branchmen know this too
> For stiffs won't talk so men must walk
> The floor without a shoe.

Part of the technique was to allow prisoners to hear others
tortured:

> I heard the moans and dreadful groans
> They rose from some man's cell.
> And knew I then that this poor friend
> Had something big to tell.
> I'd heard him go some hours ago
> His step was smooth and light,
> But he'd come back like crippled wreck
> Or one who'd lost a fight.

Bobby had given his particulars and declined to give any further information unless in the presence of his solicitor. The police refused to accept this plea and decided to beat the information out of him. There were two two-hour interrogations during which he was repeatedly punched, kicked, beaten. There was an interval and the police started again:

I was brought into a new room where there were two new detectives awaiting me. This was the third interrogation and was to prove worse than the other two. A detective stood behind me and one on the other side of the table. The detective to my left had been drinking and was very agressive and violent. 'Before you leave here you will talk .....' he said .... After each question the detective who had the drink would slap me heavily on the head, ear or face ... This sort of thing went on for half-an-hour roughly with kicks and punches thrown in occasionally. I was spread-eagled against the wall and my feet spread apart and back as far as I could manage. The detective who was reeking with alcohol was punching me in the kidneys, sides, back, neck, in fact everywhere. The other detective was holding me by the hair and firing questions into my face .... I was told to sit down, given a cigarette and soft soaped with promises, deals, etc.

> They have their means and dirty schemes
> To loosen up your tongue,
> Some talk so sweet you'd think their feat
> Was one of pleasant fun.
> But soon you learn and soon you yearn
> For safety of the cell,
> For what was thought was penance taught
> Was but the gates of hell.

Suddenly the physical torture started again:

While the detective sat in front of me he was swinging his foot and kicking me in the privates. I fell twice only to be hauled to my feet in the same position.

> They chop your neck, then walk your back
> Spread-eagled you like pelt.
> For private parts their special arts
> Are sickeningly felt.
> They squeeze them tight with no respite
> 'Till a man cries for the womb

That gave him birth to this cruel earth
And torture of that room.

That same person – continues Bobby – was chopping me on the back or
the neck, the individual blows heavy and continuous, about twenty or
thirty times. I am not sure as the other detective was punching me in the
stomach and yelling questions .... I was given another cigarette and
asked if I was all right and told it was early yet, so I could make it
shorter and easier for myself if I just put my name to a piece of paper ....
I had been interrogated and beaten for about seven hours ... When I was
told I was going back to my cell I asked to see a doctor, but they just
laughed and said, 'You have some chance.' They also said, 'So has your
fucking solicitor.'

Now some will say in sweetest way
They do not wish you harm,
They try to coax, they try to hoax
They murder you with charm.
They give you smokes they crack you jokes
Allaying all your fears,
Then beg you sign that awful line
To get you thirty years.

Bobby's narrative continues:

I was brought down the stairs into the interrogation building again. This
interrogation lasted about two hours and was followed by another which
lasted two hours. During both of these I was slapped, punched,
threatened etc ... After dinner at about 3.00 p.m. I was taken to the last
room of the interrogation building ... I was set upon by two detectives.
I was punched very heavily across the head, ears, face and eyes. I was
kicked on the legs. My head was smashed against a wooden wall .....
After this beating I was told to sit down ..... I was given a cigarette as if
nothing had happened ... I was then told that what I got was only a taste
of what I would get unless I gave the right answers to their questions ... I
was hauled out of my seat and spread-eagled against the wall. Again I
was beaten all over .... I was then thrown down on the floor and told to
do press ups. I refused. I was kicked several times so I started doing
press ups. I was only able to do three or four. I just lay down. I was
then hauled up beaten and beaten and beaten. I was disorientated .... my
two arms were twisted up my back for about ten minutes or maybe
longer. I don't know what position they were in but they were being
held together by just one person at one time while the other concentrated
on hitting me. When my arms were released from this position I could
just bring them down round to my front.
　　　I was spread-eagled again but I fell right away every time because

my arms were so painful .... I was made to stand with my eyes closed and punched in different places where I was not expecting to be hit. The interrogation ended at approximately 5.00 p.m. .... I was put back in the cell exhausted and in pain. The bright light still shone and the four walls depressed me. I got off the bed and walked up and down the cell, four paces each way. I was exhausted, pained, depressed and demoralised but I knew that if I didn't keep walking and keep my mind going that I would break down and sign my name to a lot of things I knew nothing about. I had been asked to put my signature on a blank sheet which I refused.

I was taken out that night again. I cannot remember whether it was once or twice but I do remember an interrogation at 10.00 or 10.30 p.m. It lasted one and a half hours roughly. I remember the time as one of the detectives said he wanted to get home to see Match of the Day on TV.

This last chilling sentence reminds one of the people like Eichmann and Heydrich and the SS guards in the concentration camps who went home to listen to the radio or go to a concert with their wives and families after a day of torturing others, and who reported for work the next morning to do the same thing. Incidentally, this account of Bobby's has already been published in two newspapers and in many books and to my knowledge has never been refuted.

This whole question of torture of defenceless Irish prisoners, of which Bobby Sands was only one of thousands, is the direct result of instructions from the British government which said in effect: *Get convictions no matter how.*

In 1978 the European Commission of Human Rights found Britain guilty of 'torture' (but the Court later changed this to 'inhuman and degrading treatment') of Irish prisoners. Anmesty International found the same. A number of English television programmes exposed this torture. Hundreds of signed and witnessed statements of torture have been published. Details of much of this is also given in an excellent Penguin book *Beating the Terrorists* by Peter Taylor which explains why the torture was not stopped and exposes the subsequent political cover-up. The Association of Police Surgeons of Northern Ireland protested strongly against this torture and one of their leading members Dr Robert Irwin resigned. In 1977 a statement given by thirty Northern Ireland solicitors to Roy Mason the then secretary for the north, said: 'Ill-treatment of suspects by police officers with the object of obtaining confessions is now common practice.'

An editorial of the *Irish Press* as early as 1972 strongly condemned this torture:

The men who play out the role of torturers in the north today cannot be excused. It is not enough that they are obeying orders, acting within instructions. They are guilty and should pay for their crimes. But what of the responsibility of those further up the line? The doctors and the generals, the official lawyers, and the civilian officials are also involved. And most of all the political leaders in whose interest and with whose authority these barbarities are perpetrated.

No political prisoner, particularly one extradited by Mr Haughey appearing before one of the courts in Northern Ireland has much of a chance. There are several reasons for this:

1. *The Judges:* A majority of the judges were either members of the Orange Order or ex-members of the Unionist administration. Unfortunately many of these men brought their bigotry on to the bench with them.

2. *Evidence of the Police:* The evidence of the police or the army is usually accepted as being the correct evidence despite any contrary evidence put forward by independent witnesses. In practice this means that the word of a man in uniform has become in effect the law in Northern Ireland.

3. *Acceptance of dubious evidence:* If a statement of guilt signed by the prisoner is put in evidence by the police then that evidence is usually accepted as correct. If a statement of non-guilt is put in evidence by the prisoner's solicitor then that statement is rejected. One procedure adopted by the police is to torture a man until he signs his name at the end of a blank sheet of paper – then they later type in whatever incriminating details they wish. If a prisoner produces medical evidence that he was tortured that evidence is usually rejected and the evidence of the police that there was no torture accepted. In one poem Bobby Sands wrote:

The case was clear cut, cruel by fear
And carved by hand of law
The hidden hand that choked a man
His signature to draw.

While torturous screams haunt poor men's dreams
From deeds that no one saw.

The figures show that 80% of convictions were obtained by a statement of guilt signed by prisoners. This is by far the highest in the world and nobody believes that prisoners in the six counties are queuing up to hand in signed statements of their guilt! To show the preposterous lengths to which this kind of thing can go I quote the case of a young nationalist girl. The evidence produced against the girl was her 'signed' statement admitting murder. *But this girl was illiterate.* This was proven in court yet the 'signed' statement was accepted as evidence and she was given a sentence of imprisonment.

4. *Establishment of guilt:* Unlike all other courts in the free, civilised democracies, in the six counties a Nationalist prisoner is generally presumed guilty. There is no onus on the police to prove it. However, the onus is on the prisoner to prove his innocence. In one of his poems Bobby Sands wrote:

They do adhere to law, I mused,
But that law is their own,
It is a law unto itself
Whose face is never shown.
But I have seen it, yes I have
And brunt of it I've known.

5. *Degrees of brutality:* Different judges allow different degrees of brutality as a means of obtaining signed statements. For example, one judge might allow punches, kicks, and hair-pulling while not allowing thumb screws and punching on the face. A typical example of how that works is as follows: A prisoner may show that in ten different interrogations he was tortured during eight of them. The judge may then say: 'I will not accept in evidence what you said during the eight interrogations. I will, however, accept as evidence what you said in the last two. I sentence you to fifteen years.' Bobby's poem is here revealing:

'My Lord, I gave him pleasantries
I gave him cups of tea,
I even begged him to confess

Upon my bended knee.
And after some more pleasantries
My Lord, he did agree.'

'Sergeant, there seems to be some claim
That you forced him to confess,
And that you walked upon his spine
And beat him up no less?'
'No! No! My Lord, that was his own
Self-inflicted mess!'

6. *Variation in sentence:* Another very unpleasant aspect of these courts is the difference in sentences given to Nationalist and Unionist prisoners. Some examples are: A Nationalist boy gets fifteen years for having possession of a bomb. A Unionist gets a suspended sentence for possession of arms. A Nationalist gets seventeen years for setting fire to an empty bus. A Unionist gets ten years for murder. A British soldier who murders and rapes a girl gets off free. There are hundreds of these examples. Indeed one can only describe as extraordinary the fact that the cases brought to court against members of the army and police resulted in an almost one hundred per cent acquittal. This must be a world record!

7. *Collective responsibility:* If there are six people in a house and one of them has a gun and hides it all six can get up to twenty years imprisonment for possession – even though five of these had no idea there was a gun in the house in the first place. This has been used extensively to send whole groups of Nationalists to prison for long periods, and it has been stated that in many cases the police planted the gun in the first place.

These courts, known as Diplock from the recommendations of the Diplock Commission, are not regarded by the Nationalists as courts where justice is administered but simply as conveyor belts to send as many Nationalists as quickly as possible to jail. There is now a movement to have three Diplock judges instead of one. This will probably be granted but it is all eyewash. Does anyone suggest that three Unionist judges are more just than one! It is to this kind of regime that Mr Haughey has now decided to extradite our citizens.

They can expect the same beatings, the same torture, the same prison sentences as those in the past. Is there any nation in the world that would extradite its citizens to such a criminal regime? Most extraordinary of all is that Haughey knows what exactly is in store for Irishmen and women extradited to the north and yet he continues to do so and indeed makes the 'whole system workable' as he promised Thatcher, in case it was not working to her satisfaction.

In supporting this criminal regime we not only revile the millions of Irishmen and women who were slaughtered in the past, but we revile humanity itself. This terrible regime had the backing of the British government who in the 1930s and early 1940s were condemning a similar regime in Germany, but ignoring it within their own jurisdiction. The Nationalist population had nowhere to turn. Plea after plea to the British fell on deaf ears. But far worse was the fact that similar heart-rending pleas for help to the southern Ireland government were rejected too. No Irish politician ever took any real effective steps to help their suffering, persecuted brethren in the north. (It was my mistake to believe that Haughey would.) This is a hard, cold, unpalatable *realpolitik* truth which we will run up against again and again. These politicians did not seem to want a united Ireland that would upset the rule of party politics in Dáil Éireann. They were quite prepared to make grandiloquent, verbose and stirring speeches, but everything ended with the last full stop.

Most of these unfortunate people were Catholics but again the leaders of their Church did little of practical value to help them. They did not openly side with the Unionists and they certainly disapproved of much of what the Unionists were doing, but they confined their activities to speechmaking, and to sermons advising their flock to turn the other cheek. Now, of course, most of them have come out on the side of the British. The spiritual mind, which is that of Christ Jesus, has been abandoned and has been replaced by the ecclesiastical mind, between which there is a world of difference.

The leaders of all the Protestant Churches made no protest of any kind but on the contrary they fully acquiesced in the injustices of the Unionist regime. It is therefore little wonder that the Nationalists of today treat with searing cynicism the orations of these gentlemen after sixty-seven years of silence.

A sample of the double-think of the Protestant bishops was well illustrated at the recent Lambert Conference in July – August 1988. The conference passed a resolution stating that in certain circumstances the use of violence was justified. Panic ensued amongst the pro-British elements who immediately rushed through another resolution which in effect said that the terms of the first resolution did not apply to violence in Nothern Ireland. What the ordinary person read into this was that in certain circumstances one could use violence for political ends *but not against the British*. Britain's interests were now recognised as a moral law. It is difficult to see how any rational being could have confidence in such a group of people. The consoling factor however is that in the present world what a conference of bishops decides is simply irrelevant.

For long years this besieged people tried every peaceful means to improve their lot, to eke out even a hand-to-mouth existence, but they were met only by brutality and repression from the Unionist government, contempt from the British, apathy from the Irish government and Irish politicians and indifferences from their Church. They felt themselves isolated and alone.

Two stark unpalatable truths stared them in the face. Firstly, they saw they would have to help themselves. No one would take any real practical steps to help them. Secondly, it became painfully clear that little would be achieved by peaceful means. They had tried and failed and now they saw their only hope in violence. So skilfully has the brainwashing of the public been carried out that only the thoughtful minority have seen the unpalatable fact that violence was the last resort of a people beaten almost into insensibility.

Fifty years of suffering and oppression had exhausted their patience. In 1969 they took to the streets in their thousands armed only with sticks and stones. The reign of violence had begun. The Provisional IRA was born.

FOUR

TERRORISTS OR FREEDOM FIGHTERS?

Give shelter to those who come to you. Give them help, money and anything else that might be useful to them. Let the people of the six counties know you are with them.

— NEIL BLANEY TD

We make an unprecedented appeal to the grass roots of Fianna Fáil to face up to the challenge of British rule in Ireland ... to assert that British politicians – not the Irish people – are the root cause of division and conflict in our country.

— IRA STATEMENT 1987

Garret Fitzgerald's father and his comrades shot RIC policemen. That is how they came to power, through the shooting of Catholic RIC policemen who were propping up the British state in Ireland.

— OWEN CARRON 1981

Sometimes a film on television is preceded by a warning that it may disturb viewers. I feel I should similarly sound a warning at the beginning of this chapter since much of what it contains may be as disturbing to my readers as it was to me when I first discovered the truth.

The success of the IRA has struck a kind of terror into the British so that their first major task is to destroy them in order that they may get on with the construction of defence bases in the six counties and gradually extend their influence into the Republic. The IRA constitute the one big obstacle to the promulgation of that policy. Because of this they have spent vast sums of money projecting the catchphrases: *The IRA are terrorist not freedom-fighters,* and due to the high degree of support from the media of both countries they have been very successful in persuading the public at large into accepting this catchphrase. Because of the somewhat uncritical attitude of much of the media it might be no harm if we stripped this catchphrase down a bit, ignored for a moment the skilful propaganda, the entrenched prejudices, the cynical holding on to power, and had a look at the hard, cold facts, which frankly are disturbing.

Probably the best point from which to start would be a theological one. Christian theology suggests that a revolution can be justified on three grounds:
1. If grave injustice prevails.
2. If constitutional means have been tried and failed.
3. If there is a reasonable chance of success.

How far does the present IRA campaign in the six counties fulfil these three conditions?

The injustice that prevails in the six counties is as bad, and in some cases worse, than in any oppressed country in the world. Indeed these conditions of injustice are much more acute than the conditions prevailing in 1916 and that revolution, although initially condemned, has now been blessed with theological approval. The commemorative services are graced by the highest ecclesiastics in the land, both Catholic and Protestant.

The two previous chapters in this book show that the most blatant and obnoxious injustice has prevailed and is prevailing in the six counties. There is a strong resemblance between it and the treatment in Nazi occupied countries during the Second World War where so many gallant resistance fighters fought to end this injustice. By no stretch of imagination could the six county state be described as a democracy. Murder, shoot-to-kill, torture, discrimination, harassment are unfortunately the norm so that an unbiased observer can only come to the conclusion that the first condition justifying a revolution exists here.

What of the second condition?

Unfortunately constitutional means of every kind have been tried for more than sixty years and have failed. Those who sincerely attempted such means were brutalised, jailed, treated with absolute contempt. Even today organisations like the SDLP are ignored and treated like recalcitrant children who are tolerated so long as they do not go too far. These terrible conditions were summarised by Bernadette McAliskey in a lecture some time ago:

> They told us to use the democratic process and we used it. We used it way back in 1918, we used it when Bobby Sands was dying, and Sinn Féin have used it since. But there is a problem with the democratic process. If you elect people which the government think are not suitable, they scurry like rats into the House of Commons and pass a law saying you are allowed to elect people of your choice as long as you do not elect people of the following calibre. If you elect those people then we will pretend you didn't ...
>
> We have a problem with operating within the law, not simply because they change it all the time but because they have now taken their politics right into the courts ... We were born guilty.
>
> We are part of an Irish community who were historically forced to live within a state whose legality and whose right to exist we have never ever conceded. We live in *a country where all that is brave, good, idealistic and hopeful is in jail. All that is underhand, petty, mean and dishonest is in power* (Italic mine).

Any independent observer will not find it hard to discover that constitutional politics have achieved almost nothing and there is no evidence to suggest that it is likely to achieve anything in the future. It has been tried over and over again and failed. It is being tried today with no success. The track record of British injustice all over the world shows that they do not yield to constitutional means.

Here again it seems clear that the second condition for a theologically justified revolution exists.

The third condition is that there must be a reasonable hope of success. Again the facts speak for themselves. The IRA have conducted one of the longest guerrilla campaigns ever against the British who now publicly admit they cannot beat them. General James Glover, who was commander of the British army in the six counties, said recently on TV that the IRA could *not* be militarily defeated. 'In no way can or will the Provisional IRA ever be defeated militarily.' He said: 'The campaign would go on as long as the Provisional IRA have the stamina, the political motivation to sustain their campaign and so long as there is a divided island of Ireland.'

So, if they keep it up they are likely to succeed one day and that very idea terrifies southern politicians almost as much as the British.

The present IRA would argue that their campaign fulfils these conditions and that theologically speaking they are *waging a just war* and it would be difficult to deny their claim.

All this, of course, is a very hard and bitter fact to accept especially in the light of the propaganda about terrorists but all the propaganda in the world cannot suppress truth permanently.

At this point I should say that I have no desire to spend my remaining years in an Irish jail. Because of our most repressive legislation a nod in the direction of the IRA could get one five or ten years. So I want to make quiet clear that nothing in this book is intended to promote or help illegal organisations. It is merely a statement of facts. I did not invent the theological conditions for a just revolution. These are the work of St Thomas Aquinas who is lucky to be dead. Otherwise he might be charged under the Offences Against the State Act, and find himself in jail.

All this, however, is not to approve of some of the methods they use in waging this war, but in the theological sense and in the abstract they have a just and valid reason to fight the British. So before condemning them we should try at least to understand their point of view. Against this it has been argued that many bishops have opposed the IRA and would condemn their war on theological grounds. Few people, however, would pay much attention to what the bishops have to say. Their long history in Ireland has shown them not to be over concerned with justice – rather are they concerned with structures, with position and with power and almost without exception they sided with the British and put questions of justice discreetly to one side. Their views for the most part carry little weight today either at home or in Rome.

In opposition to the bishops' attitude is that of one of the north's most prominent priests, Fr Joseph McVeigh:

I don't see the IRA as criminal. I see them as very motivated, highly idealistic people who are prepared to sacrifice their own lives for the greater good. When the government engages in brutality they respond in the only way they can ...

The one way out is not for the IRA to lay down their arms. The only way is for the British government to declare their intention to withdraw. Every generation has resorted to arms to resist the British. Every generation will continue to do so.

And together with another priest, Fr Des Wilson, they said:

> After careful consideration we are convinced that the present course which has been adopted by the Catholic Hierarchy is both erroneous and dangerous ... We would contend that many of the recent pronouncements of our bishops have been politically motivated.

What these priests have to say represents but the tip of the iceberg. Quite a substantial number of other priests would agree with them, such as the great Fr McDyer who, shortly before his death, told me that he saw the IRA as having right on their side. But these men rarely get an opportunity to put forward their views. How many times have we seen them on TV? The number of times would contrast rather strangely with the regularity with which we see Unionists and SDLP politicians presenting their worn-out views.

The present IRA are also being loudly condemned by almost everyone of standing in the community; public officials, academics, politicians, the media etc. I find it intriguing to read in the old newspapers that it was the same categories of people who condemned Pearse, De Valera and others during the Anglo-Irish war. More interesting still is the fact that the very words which these people are using today 'thugs, murderers, terrorists, criminals' are the same words which were used half a century ago to describe individuals who a short time later were to be revered as men of the highest honour and integrity. There is something here that does not quite add up. If these men of the past were really criminals how could they all miraculously turn into saints a few months or a few years later? Or could there be some truth in Napoleon's remark that 'God is on the side of the victors'? Is it possible that the IRA of today, now condemned as terrorists, may at some future date be

respected as men of uprightness and rectitude? Has this not
happened before and could it not happen again? Could it
really be that the standards by which Irish critics judge people
and events are such that they can be trimmed to suit every
wind? Or could it be said that I am too cynical if I suspect that
there must be mountains of hypocrisy around – that justice
counts for nothing and that power and greed count for
everything? As Solzhenitsyn says: 'The truth is seldom sweet;
it is almost invariably bitter.'

The harsh reality is, of course, that the present day IRA see
themselves as the inheritors of the ideals of Pearse, Connolly
and Collins – ideals which have been abandoned by successive
Irish governments both of Fianna Fáil and Coalition and, I
suspect, that is the reason they are hated so much. Isn't it
somewhat a pity that the actual statements made by the IRA
are not sufficiently aired on our media? The following
important statement was issued as far back as 1973:

Will talk achieve more than the gun? Yes, definitely yes. And the IRA
are more than willing to talk. We have said many times that we detest
this war with its suffering and misery. We would much rather settle our
differences in a civilised way. It is the British, not we, who still refuse
to negotiate.

Again and again Danny Morrison's famous speech about the
'armalite and the ballot box' has been highlighted. What has
not been highlighted, however, are the other words he used.

We are a peaceful people. I repeat we are a peaceful people. But it needs
to be said fearlessly because it is the truth: after what we have come
through for fifty years, the repression, the discrimination .... it's no
crime and there's no moral wrong in lifting a stone, planting a bomb,
raising a rifle against those who repress our people.

One IRA member said to Vincent Browne of *Magill* magazine:

You have to remember that life in the IRA is no bed of roses. There are
no rich Provos. We have to suffer imprisonment, torture, being
constantly on the run, isolated from our families ..... There is also the
factor of being constantly misrepresented and condemned by the
supposed moral leaders of our society.

One of the recent ploys used by the British has been to feed false information to the Irish government that the IRA have designs to make war on the Republic and that the Irish should make one cause with the British in crushing the IRA. Haughey and his cabinet seem to have fallen for this ploy in spite of regular statements from the IRA that such is not the case. All members of the IRA have instructions not to engage in conflict with the security forces of the Republic. But it seems as if Dublin prefers to believe the British version.

When I was researching some of my writings on the six counties, I spoke with many IRA people – those currently being termed 'thugs, murderers and criminals'. I was conditioned to expect a kind of seedy cross between Bill Sykes and Al Capone. The reality turned out to be quite different. Those with whom I spoke were reasonable, intelligent and dedicated young men. They would much prefer to live a normal life but this was denied them and they had come to the end of the road, to the point where they believed that only the gun produced results. Again and again they quized me as to what I would personally do if I had been treated as they and their families were. Again and again I funked the answer. Responsible elements within the British army itself privately admitted to admiring their dedication and self-sacrifice while publicly condemning them. There was nothing very secretive about them except their whereabouts. Unlike TDs and ministers none of them were in the £20,000 to £100,000 a year a bracket. In fact I doubt if any of them had little more than pocket money. They spoke freely to me and answered my questions, even though, with my background, they had no reason to trust me too far. In trying to help me many ran great personal risks.

Unlike the SDLP, Sinn Féin are not prepared to give any allegiance to the British crown. SDLP members elected to the British parliament are obliged to make the following declaration:

I ...... solemnly, sincerely and truly declare and affirm that I will be faithful and bear true allegiance to Her Majesty Queen Elizabeth, her heirs and successors, according to law.

What does that mean? It seems to me that they are giving

their 'true allegiance' to the symbol of one of the most brutal and undemocratic nations in the world. What would have happened to politicians in occupied countries who declared publicly their allegiance to Hitler? Gerry Adams has refused to make that declaration and therefore cannot take his seat and draw his £25,000 a year salary.

It is at this point that many readers might expect me to pose the rather self-righteous question: How could such reasonable men carry out the killings they have?

To those seeking an answer to this question, perhaps they should ask the SAS who carried out the Gibraltar and Loughall killings, the security forces who conducted the shoot-to-kill policy along the border, or the British paratroopers who carried out the Bloody Sunday killings. These experts could probably provide the best answers.

I am not trying to defend the IRA and what they do. I am merely presenting the facts and suggesting that before condemning them one should try to understand them. I have noticed that those who condemn them most loudly do so from the safety and comfort of their homes, their offices, their armchairs. Few of them have ever had their doors smashed in by the butt of a rifle or their homes raided in the middle of the night.

On a personal note may I say that I know what I am talking about. As a captain in the army helping the gardaí, I broke down doors with the butt of a rifle and pulled young IRA men at gunpoint from their beds in the early hours of the morning, in front of their screaming mothers, wives and children. I too believed they were 'terrorists'. I did so because I never enquired too closely into what I was told and what the media was saying. It was only when I decided to think for myself and investigate that I came upon the truth.

To crush and destroy the IRA is what the British want because it gives them domination over the six counties. Is that what Haughey wants? Is that what the grass roots of Fianna Fáil want?

Whether we like it or not we have to face the reality of the IRA. They are there to stay and like the old IRA they will not give up until they have achieved a withdrawal of the British.

In helping the British to crush the IRA Haughey is trying to silence the one voice of nationalism left in Ireland. He is unlikely to succeed. All the chances are that they will outlast him and that people like Bobby Sands will be respected long after Haughey's name has been forgotten.

Would it not be better if he just left them alone? Neither helped them or obstructed them? They are no threat to the Republic. Unfortunately he seems to have been 'conned' into playing the role of Britain's policeman and jailer at a cost of £500,000,000 per year. One expects that from Fine Gael but not from Fianna Fáil.

It is of interest to note that Britain too spends £500,000,000 on security in the north – that is between them one billion pounds is spent annually – and they cannot defeat a few hundred dedicated men and women.

What useful purposes could all that money be put to if Britain ceased her colonialism and if Haughey ceased to help her? Here again we sense the truth of the old Irish proverb: *It's easy to sleep on another man's wound,* and also the validity of the old eastern proverb: *Trust but verify.*

All my life I have tried in my own small way to live by the principles of truth and justice, but truth I have found particularly hard to find. So many people, especially politicians and members of the establishment have a vested interest in falsehood and lies, particularly the fundamental lie that Britain has a right to be in the six counties. These people have at their disposal large sums of money to promulgate such falsehoods so that ordinary people are overwhelmed and impressed. Every time I think of these people and their cold-blooded cynicism I find it hard to restrain my anger and fury. At times I yearn for the burning words of a Zola or a Swift to condemn and denounce them from the hilltop, because I cannot help thinking, and I must say it, that they are the real villains. But I know my protest will be of no avail. As the years pass some of them will be graciously received in Buckingham Palace and have titles conferred upon them. Others here at home will be honoured by university degrees honoris causa. All will live out their lives on most liberal pensions, laden down with honours, though not with honour, and it is unlikely that they will ever spare a thought for the thousands of Irish men and women and children who were sent to early graves either directly or indirectly through their political errors and greed. That thought alone is sufficient to make the most hardened agnostic believe in a Day of General Judgement.

FIVE

THE FINAL INSULTS

The British never commit a useless crime. When they hire a man to assassinate an Irish Patriot, when they blow a Sepoy [Indian] from the mouth of a cannon, when they produce a famine in one of their dependencies, they always have an ulterior motive .... Every crime the English have planned and carried out in Ireland has had a definite end.
— PÁDRAIG PEARSE

The analogy with the Nazis is real. The systems which have resulted in the destruction of a people are in operation in Northern Ireland.
— US SOCIOLOGIST, RONA FIELDS

You are a lot of bloodthirsty collaborators with the British ... You are rolling over on your back in order that Mrs Thatcher will tickle your tummys, as a BBC commentator described you.
— NEIL BLANEY TD, IN DÁIL ÉIREANN, MARCH 1988

In my book *The Statesman* I expressed the view that Haughey was the leader most likely to stand up to the British and make Irishmen and women hold their heads on high again.

Re-reading today what I wrote I am flabbergasted that I could have been so naive, that I could have believed in him and trusted him despite warning lights flashing from all sides. That I should have asked thousands of my readers to do the same is unforgivable.

Up to the very last I held out hope. I clutched at every straw to bolster up the foolishness I had written, but in the winter-spring of 1987-1988 a series of incidents happened that proved beyond all doubt that my thesis in *The Statesman* was hopelessly wrong. It is worth having a look at these incidents.

Enniskillen

Despite media hype it is not known as yet what happened at Enniskillen. The British version is that the IRA placed a bomb which was to be detonated at the moment when the crowd was largest, thus causing the maximum number of casualties.

The IRA version is that they placed the bomb in an old building which they had reason to believe would be searched by the security forces several hours before the actual ceremony. They intended to detonate it during the search and inflict severe casualties on the British security forces. Something quite extraordinary then happened. Although other buildings in the vicinity were searched, *the one containing the bomb was not.* As to why this was not searched no satisfactory explanation has been given. The IRA say the British knew the bomb was there, did not search the building and then when the crowd was assembled detonated it by remote control so that the IRA would be blamed and public revulsion would follow thus easing the way for extradition. They had done this before in Dublin killing a number of people and this facilitated the passing of the Offences Against the State Act. Only time alone will tell which of the two versions is the correct one and it is not within the orbit of this book to determine the answer. One should, however, not forget the words of Fr Faul in 1982: 'I can verify that the British never told the truth about a single incident in Northern Ireland since 1970.'

What is, however, of great relevance here is Haughey's reaction to Enniskillen. Because of the serious doubt about what actually happened at Enniskillen one would have expected Haughey to heed Fr Faul's words and wait for confirmation. This would have been the kind of ordinary prudence any statesman would exercise, but instead Haughey plumped immediately for the British version, despite his knowledge and experience of British untruthfulness in the past. It was as if he were over-reaching himself to please them. The first thing he did was to send a message of sympathy to Mrs Thatcher. This is quite significant because by this action he fully acknowledged her jurisdiction over the six counties and in doing so acknowledged the six counties as British, not Irish. He could have sent a message to the Chairman of the Enniskillen Urban Council, which would not have compromised our constitutional position, but he chose not to do so. This impulsive action is surely a pointer to his thinking.

As a direct result he renewed Section 31 of the Broadcasting Act even though the Fianna Fáil Ard Fheis had voted overwhelmingly against renewing it, but paying attention to what Fianna Fáil delegates say is not one of Haughey's strong points.

He then rushed into the biggest search ever in the history of the Irish state known as *Operation Mallard* but nicknamed *Operation Bullshit* by *Phoenix* magazine.

It is worth while taking a closer look at this search since it brought to a new height the level of co-operation between Haughey and the security forces in the north – a level which even Fitzgerald or Cosgrave never reached.

Operation Mallard was a widespread search which lasted more than a week in November 1987 in which thousands of Irish homes were searched, in most cases, without search warrants. There is reason to believe it was prompted by the British who fed the story that a number of shiploads of arms landed at various points on our coast. There is no evidence whatever for this story. The source is two-fold: (1) M16 of the British Secret Service, not exactly the fountainhead of truth, and (2) the French Secret Service who blew up the Greenpeace ship and then denied it – hardly a fountainhead of truth either. On the basis of this information, which not even a child would accept without some verification, Haughey initiated the raids. He also accepted the British version of the *Eksund* without any proof as to where those arms were destined to go.

The operation was co-ordinated with the RUC and British army who carried out complementary raids on Nationalist homes in the north at the same time. A week before this operation an RUC officer visited Dublin and made an offer of modern detection equipment. It was, of course, really the British who were making this offer and they were suggesting that they would send their own men down to operate it. The offer of equipment was accepted but whether the British operated it in conjunction with the gardaí south of the border is unknown.

The last time we borrowed equipment from the British to use against Irishmen was during the shelling of the Four Courts in 1922. It was hardly imagined then that a future leader, Charles Haughey, of the party that emerged from the ashes of the Four Courts – Fianna Fáil – would use British equipment against the homes of members of that party. It is unlikely that Haughey offered any explanation to the grass roots of the party why Fianna Fáil had to be associated with this Irish-British operation.

As it turned out the search was a fiasco, no arms worthwhile were found, because the landing stories were false, and it cost the Irish taxpayer between £1,000,000 and £2,000,000, at a time when the old and poor were suffering severe health cuts.

There is still about £1,000,000 worth of this equipment in the hands of the gardaí on what was described as long term loan. The British have offered to provide 'civilian' personnel to run the equipment on future raids. Here one has to be very careful with the word 'civilian'. It has been known in the past that some of these civilians have been M16 personnel in disguise. Judging by our track record we are probably stupid enough to fall for that one too. One should remember the Russian proverb: *Don't call a wolf to help you against the dogs.* All in all, through *Operation Mallard*, the British have out-witted and out-manoeuvred Haughey once again. Not so good for Fianna Fáil, however, is the news that a large number of supporters say they will not vote for the party again because many of their homes were raided. I have spoken to scores of life long supporters of Fianna Fáil who say they will never vote for the party again. They would prefer to abstain or vote for Independents with no transfers. If this happens then Fianna Fáil could be out of office for a long time.

Enniskillen raises another interesting point. Here British interests were damaged and Haughey took *action* on every front. British interests were damaged when an Irish court refused to extradite Patrick McVeigh. Haughey immediately jumped to *action* by appealing the decision to the High Court. He also wrote at once to Mrs Thatcher. What was in that letter? Would he care to reveal the contents to the Fianna Fáil grass roots? Let us now look at some incidents where Irish interests were damaged and we will see that Haughey's response took the form of *words*, not actions.

The Stalker Affair

In 1985 a book called *Shoot to Kill?* was published. It was the authoritative report of the International Lawyers' Inquiry into the lethal use of firearms by the security forces in the six counties. Professor Kadar Asmal of Trinity College was the chairman and editor of the book. This distinguished commission of international lawyers found, among other things, as follows:

The evidence we have heard leads us to conclude that an administrative practice has been allowed to develop in Northern Ireland, by which killings in violation of the European Convention and the International Covenant are at least tolerated if not actually encouraged. Undercover units of the British army and the RUC are trained to shoot to kill even where killing is not legally justified and where alternative tactics could be used. Such administrative practices are illegal in domestic and international law. They should be stopped and training for them should be discontinued immediately.

In conclusion we find that the misuse of firearms by the security forces in Northern Ireland is part of a broader pattern of human rights violations which has led to a serious breakdown in public confidence in the administration of justice generally ...

We consider that the Government of Ireland as a party to the European Convention would be justified in bringing an interstate application to the European Commission on Human Rights under Article 24 of the Convention alleging violation of Article 2 and Article 13.

Despite the fact that large sections of the media ignored this book it became an instant success and at the present moment is enjoying a steady sale. What this all adds up to is that years before the Stalker Affair this distinguished body of lawyers found evidence of a 'shoot-to-kill' policy operating in the north. Haughey was made aware of the policy then. I know because I personally sent him a copy of the book *Shoot to Kill?* the day it was published.

The Stalker-Sampson Report is believed to confirm what

was by then well known. It is believed, however, that it contained one extra section of vital information, namely the infiltration of the gardaí by the British Secret Service and the cross-border incursions by British 'shoot-to-kill' gangs. Haughey and the government were made aware of all this. They knew the names of the gardaí involved in helping M16 and in helping SAS terrorists to cross the border. This information had come to them from impeccable sources. This I know because I was indirectly involved in the provision of some of this information. Why then all the fuss about the Stalker-Sampson report when the government already knew the main thrust of what it contained?

The British Attorney-General, Mayhew, a man not unacquainted with insensitivity, decided not to prosecute those security officers involved in the shoot-to-kill policy and in the miscarriage of justice. He did not in fact have to release any part of the report. He could have said, 'We have received the report but in the interests of national security we will not give any details,' and despite a few protests the matter would have ended. Instead he chose a course which on the face of it looks highly provocative. He admitted that some of the officers were part of a perversion of justice but announced that he would not prosecute them. He did not have to make that pronouncement which, as anyone could have foreseen, caused an outcry of indignation.

It seems quite a likely explanation that this was a cabinet decision to test Haughey's mettle and see how far they could go. Haughey could have taken many courses of action. He could have issued proceedings against Britain in the international court. This would have been highly embarrassing to the British in a world wide context. He could again have said 'No extradition to such a regime.' Instead he chose to do nothing except verbalise the matter. He said:

We have also indicated in our public statement our concern that it can have serious implications for cross-border co-operation.

That statement is virtually meaningless. He speaks of 'our concern'. What does that mean? Does it mean that he is 'concerned' that he may not be able to help the British enough? Why did he not use the words 'it *will* have serious consequences' instead of 'can have'. For a wishy-washy milk-and-water statement in time of national crisis it would be hard to beat – for it was a national crisis. What the British were saying in effect was: 'We will shoot who we like, where we like and when we like and we don't care a fig about what you think', and they later implemented that policy. Notice here that although he had many *practical* options open to him he chose the ineffectual *verbal* one. They had met mush, not steel, and decided to push on.

The Gibraltar Killings

As if to drive home to Haughey the contempt in which they held his opinions, the British carried out the most blatant killings when they shot two Irishmen and one Irish woman in Gibraltar in cold blood. These people were unarmed. They had a car in which no explosives were found. Subsequently a car was found in a Spanish car-park with explosives. This car is now believed to have been a British plant and did not belong to the three. The three could have been apprehended at any time but the British chose to kill them in cold blood. It was as if they were saying to Haughey once again: 'We will shoot who we like, when we like and where we like.'

What was Haughey's response to this? As the British guessed, it was feeble and ineffectual. The British had fired another shot across his bows and he ran for cover. He referred to these killings as 'undesirable happenings'. He would be 'represented at the inquest'. He was 'seeking full details'. He would 'consider making a fuller statement'. He was 'gravely perturbed'. This was nothing more than a pathetic barrage of verbiage – worthless, useless words. When Tony Gregory asked him if he would suspend co-operation between the gardaí and the northern security forces, he hedged and said: 'these matters were kept under constant review'. In other words nothing would be done. This British atrocity would be met with a curtain of cliches and nothing more.

It is interesting to compare here De Valera's reaction to a similar situation known as the Coventry bombings. Two young

men, Peter Barnes and James MacCormack, were sentenced to
death by a British court for the bombing. Like the Birmingham
six both of these young men were innocent. I have a particular
knowledge of this incident since I spoke at length to the man
who actually placed the bomb. On the day of their execution
De Valera declared a day of national mourning. Flags flew at
half-mast, places of public entertainment closed. Religious
services were held in various churches and the entire nation
expressed its public sympathy.

What would Haughey have done in this situation? A letter
'making our views known'?

The Release of Private Thain

Thain was convicted of the killing of a civilian and was
sentenced to life imprisonment. Some 136 Irish civilians have
been killed by the British security forces, but Thain was the
only one convicted. Having served three years of his sentence
he was released and allowed to re-join his regiment. Here
Haughey had a glorious opportunity to act and show his
mettle. He could have done as De Valera did and as John A.
Costello did and released a number of IRA prisoners. The
British could say nothing. They had released a convicted
killer so why shouldn't Haughey release at least some of those
who were not even convicted of a capital crime? The answer is,
of course, that he did not have the courage or backbone of De
Valera or Costello. Again he wilted as the British expected.
He did nothing effective and it was once more clear to the
British that they were up against mush.

The Prevention of Terrorism Act

After scoring so many victories over Haughey the British
kept pressing home their luck. They made the Prevention of
Terrorism Act – which is directed almost exclusively at the
Irish – permanent. Haughey could have reacted by stopping
the gardaí passing information, on those arrested, to the
British. But again nothing came except the usual barrage of
cliches: 'We are monitoring the situation' etc. from the
Department of Foreign Affairs. The British had won again.

The Birmingham Six

Everyone, including the British, know that these men are innocent. Even if they wanted to keep up the charade of British justice, the home secretary could still have released them on compassionate grounds like he did Private Thain. How did Haughey react? Did he put his foot down and do something practical? No, but he gave us the following piece of wish-wash in the form of one of his concerns:

.... that the home secretary consider the use of the wide-ranging powers available to him in regard to the Birmingham Six.

What an absurd, vague, spineless statement from an Irish prime minister! He did not even make a 'demand' on the home secretary. He merely pleaded with him to 'consider' taking action. What would happen if one of the Birmingham Six escaped from jail? Would Haughey extradite him? How could the British have any respect for him. Each time they threw down the gauntlet Haughey refused to pick it up.

The Belfast Shootings

After the shocked world reaction to Gibraltar the British desperately needed something to distract attention away from these killings. A very short time afterwards, a series of killings took place in Belfast. Were these killings accidental or were they planned?

It is not within the scope of this book to examine these incidents in detail and to answer that question. Nevertheless I am quite satisfied that there is a *prima facie* case that the British Secret Service had a strong input into both incidents.

The first of these incidents took place on 16 March in Milltown Cemetery, Belfast, during the burial of two of the victims of the Gibraltar killings. A lone gunman threw a number of grenades and fired several shots into the crowd of mourners, killing three young men and injuring more than sixty. A group of mourners chased him and eventually captured him near a motorway. A white van belonging to the RUC had been parked on the roadway. It sped off without making any attempt to intervene while the gunman was shooting into the crowd. The moment the gunman was captured, however, those who did so were surrounded by police and they subsequently stated that they were threatened with plastic bullet guns.

It is obviously too early yet to assess in detail what precisely happened but the statement made by Gerry Adams, MP, at a later press conference might be usefully studied since it got very little coverage in the media. Mr Adams stated:

To launch that attack those involved must have had pre-notice that there would be no RUC/British army presence, as there had been up to yesterday evening, around these funerals. We are asserting that they had pre-notice and that there was collusion.

According to AP/RN newspaper Adams pointed out that the RUC and British army enjoyed several vantage points over Milltown Cemetery and adjoining stretch of motorway.

First there was the white RUC van which would have been in constant radio contact with other RUC units and whose occupants made no attempt to intervene in contrast to the unarmed Nationalists who risked their lives to chase the gunman. At least two British helicopters were airborne, one hovering directly over the motorway. Such helicopters are fitted with sophisticated electronic surveillance apparatus as standard equipment. The attack must also have been clearly visible from the British army observation post on the top of the Broadway tower block and from the high mast-mounted cameras at Anderstown RUC barracks. Mr Adams further observed:

It took between ten and fifteen minutes for the RUC to respond to an attacker who was clearly seen throwing grenades and firing a pistol over a similar period of time. This surely contrasts with the refined two minute response that the RUC and British army have evolved to any shooting incident in Nationalist areas. Implicit in that is that the attackers were meant to escape. Only the unpredicted pursuit by Nationalist youths prevented this .... this attack could only have been effected with a tip-off from elements of the RUC to Loyalist paramilitaries.

When the dust cleared, however, the British were the winners. They had succeeded in capturing world headlines and portraying the incidents as the mad Irish killing each other while the good and noble British were trying to keep them apart.

The second of these shooting took place on Saturday 19 March during the funeral of one of the victims of the Milltown murders. An unmarked car containing two armed British soldiers in civilian dress drove straight into the funeral procession and then backed away. The car was stopped by the crowd who then set upon the soldiers, disarmed them and then shot them. These are the bones of the story which earned screaming headlines about mob rule, murder of innocents etc. It was another major propaganda victory for the British. Unfortunately most of the media accepted their viewpoint without enquiring too deeply into the matter, but there are other factors which did not receive any great publicity.

The two soldiers were said to be members of a signal corps. This was not the whole truth. They were believed to be members of the notorious SAS killer corps who carried out major killings such as Gibraltar and Loughall. They were nominally on the roll of the signal corps to give them a cover up. What were they doing driving into this funeral cortege? The mourners were convinced that there was going to be a repeat of what happened a few days previously at the Milltown funerals. They thought it was going to be another massacre and they were determined to act swiftly to prevent it. Such was the explosive atmosphere of the day.

It was subsequently alleged that a patrol of British soldiers watched from a few hundred yards away, while their two colleagues were being killed. One of them was quoted as saying that if they had gone in, which would have only taken a minute or two, the two men would have been saved. It has also been alleged that *they requested permission to do so and were refused*. If this is accurate then the implications are simply staggering. But the British are no strangers to callous killings. Alexander Solzhenitsyn, writing about Russian civilians and prisoners-of-war who did not want to return to Russia, said:

English soldiers killed Russians who did not want to become prisoners of Stalin .... British units shot, bayoneted and clubbed these people ... but for almost thirty years the free, proud and unfettered press of these two countries (America and Britain) unanimiously and with studied innocence kept silent about their government's acts of treachery.

In Italy in 1945 the British gave orders which sent over 40,000 Cossack prisoners-of-war to be slaughtered by the Russians.

With this savagery as a background what odds a few British soldiers in the six counties? Were these two men deliberately sent in to the midst of the funeral cortege so that they would be killed in order to obtain a propaganda victory? Why did their colleagues not come to their rescue? These questions remain unanswered, but what is certain is that the incident again gave the British a resounding propaganda victory and helped in a great measure to offset the world shame caused by the Gibraltar killings.

Did Haughey take any real practical action like he did after Enniskillen? Unfortunately he did not. He was 'perturbed', 'shocked', and he mustered a plethora of foreign affairs' cliches, probably to impress Fianna Fáil grass roots, but took no effective action whatsoever. The British won again.

In the meantime what emerged from these few incidents out of several was that the British were having a field day in Ireland. They now believed that they could do what they virtually liked and Haughey would not stop them. On the contrary they could count on his co-operation and support. No wonder Neil Blaney, TD, was constrained to remark in Dáil Éireann when he was refused time to comment on these things:

I am scandalised and disgraced to be in any such assembly conducted totally undemocratically and by a lot of collaborators with the British occupiers of this country which is the cause of all that you are talking about here this evening.

So too might the Fianna Fáil grass roots hang their heads in shame. The domination of this once great party by the British was now almost complete.

As if to prove that such is the case one has only to look at a statement made by Brian Lenihan, Foreign Minister, after a meeting with the British in July 1988. According to newspaper reports he said:

I have never seen the British Government so happy with the whole area of security co-operation.

Here we have the shameful situation of the Tanaiste yelping his delight that a Fianna Fáil government should have so pleased the British in the matter of helping their discredited security forces – obviously more pleased than they were with Fine Gael.

And all the while most, though not all, of the Irish media abandoned penetrating investigation and opted for sickening self-delusion.

SIX

IRELAND IN THE WILDERNESS

Leaders are the custodians of a nation's ideals, of the beliefs it cherishes, of its permanent hopes, of faith which makes a nation out of a mere aggregation of individuals.

— WALTER LEPPMAN

Power with continual acquiescence is not power at all.
— ALEXANDER SOLZHENITSYN

Nothing doth more hurt in a state than that cunning men pass for wise.
— FRANCIS BACON

In Ireland we persecute the man who rings the fire-alarm but the man who starts the fire we leave in peace.

— ANON

The Ireland of the 1980s could well be called an Ireland in the wilderness. It has lost its way rather badly in world affairs. It has scarcely one characteristic of identity that any European nation would take for granted – culture, language, self-respect. It has taken on board instead the characteristics of a banana republic subservient to a foreign power. A look at the principal characteristics of the mess that is the Ireland of today is somewhat frightening.

We are a country partly occupied, grovelling before our occupiers who are brutalising part of our population in the same way as the Nazis brutalised the countries that they occupied. To be occupied by a ruthless foreign power is no disgrace. To grovel, fawn and collaborate with that power is a disgrace of the greatest magnitude and we, the Irish of this generation, in so far as we remain inactive, are fully guilty of this debasement of ourselves. Not only that but the Irish taxpayer is forced to pay £500,000,000 per year to keep that power in occupation and there have been no 'cuts' in this field. According to an article in the *Irish Press* 'defence sources have been told by the government that the money is not a problem in the fight against paramilitaries.' In other words there is no money for hospitals, schools, unemployment, etc. but money is no object when it comes to helping the British.

In 1970 the British set out on a propaganda war to make us think British, to make us see things British as superior to our own and in this way bring about a state of affairs where they could easily dominate our political policies to their own strategic and military advantage. They specially targeted the Fianna Fáil party – they had long won over the main opposition party – and the direction of their trust was to slowly erode the Republican ideals upon which Fianna Fáil was based.

They now claim privately that they have almost succeeded in this task. The Fianna Fáil parliamentary party, they say, have abandoned the ideals of the founder and are now as close to the British as ever Fine Gael were. Not so, however, the grass roots of the party and the great British fear is that the ground swell from the rank and file may well propel a leader who could reverse the process and return Fianna Fáil to its original policies; but for the moment the British media are boasting that security co-operation under Haughey and Fianna Fáil has reached an 'unprecedented high.' This, as I have shown, was confirmed by Brian Lenihan. How long the grass roots will stand by while the ideals their founders suffered and fought for are abrogated is not so easily forecast but it is difficult to see them tolerating much longer the destruction of this great party.

In speaking to the Fianna Fáil Ard-Fheis Haughey said:

Our Republican philosophy requires us to identify where the national interest lies at any stage of the country's history and do everything in our power to protect and promote it.

Few would quibble with these sentiments until one asks the real question: Who defines the 'national interests'? – Charles Haughey or, as it appears at present, Margaret Thatcher? Certainly not the Fianna Fáil party. Up to now they have been good and truly ignored and if anyone has any doubts about that one only need look at the Ard-Fheis resolutions on the return of Neil Blaney and the ending of Section 31 and what subsequently happened.

For the past twenty years or so there has been a steady decline in the influence of the grass roots of Fianna Fáil on party policy. This has been taken over by the new style leadership, harshly referred to as the 'mohair brigade', who have little concern for party ideals, and who tend to see the grass roots as serfs to be fully utilised during election time and national collection time – work hard, pay up and above all shut up.

It would, of course, be very unfair to blame Haughey for the rot in Fianna Fáil. This set in during the leadership of Jack Lynch and is fully and frighteningly described and documented in Kevin Boland's book, *The Rise and Decline of Fianna Fáil*. He commented rather sharply on the parliamentary party:

I watched the performance particularly at government level with growing disillusionment. Here was the Republican Party (Fianna Fáil) in time of national crisis and national opportunity .... From May 1970 to November 1970 I had the opportunity to survey the parliamentary party and I was sickened by what I saw – an almost complete lack of principle – one idea only – to avoid a general election, to avoid the possibility of losing one's seat.

Here the intriguing thing is that Haughey was one of those most strongly opposed to this tendency. He was one of those opposed to the union-jacking of Fianna Fáil but why then didn't he reverse the course when he came to power and bring back Fianna Fáil to its original Republican ideals since that was the principal reason he was elected leader of the party? Above all why did he indicate in private as well as in public that this was exactly what he was going to do and then not do it? This must surely put a big question mark on his credibility.

There is, alas, no shortage of pundits who put forward various theories which purport to provide answers to Haughey's latter-day conversion to, it is alleged, the British view-point.

One theory for example says that Haughey, being the son of a 1922 Free State army officer, is basically Fine Gael in his outlook but that he joined Fianna Fáil because he believed it would give him a better chance of personal advancement: that he is a man short on ideals and principles who will go with the side most likely to be advantageous to himself. Advocates of this theory argue that Haughey now believes there are more votes to be picked up in the pro-British Fine Gael and PD sectors and that in a last analysis all he is interested in is votes. Here his critics also say that he might well try to amalgamate Fine Gael with Fianna Fáil and would be quite prepared to do so even on Fine Gael terms. He would then appear to history as one of the men who ended civil war politics. Unfortunately the lessons of history show that the complete abandonment of Republican ideals would be the perfect recipe for a new civil war. 'There is one sure way to satisfy the hunger of a tiger,' said Konrad Adenauer, 'Let him devour you!'

Of course only Haughey himself knows for certain what validity there is in this theory and it is most unlikely that he will tell us. The public will simply have to make up their own minds.

Have I made up my mind? Yes I have. My theory is a great deal simpler than any of the others. It is this: *Haughey is not able for his job as prime minister.* On the level of leadership and statesmanship he is incompetent.

That theory needs clarification. I am not saying that he is an incompetent man as such. He is incompetent only in so far as it relates to his job as prime minister. As a cabinet minister, serving under another, he was excellent. In the world of business it does not follow that a good salesman or administrator makes a good managing director. This has been proven over and over again. The qualities required for top leadership are very different than those required for executive positions. In each of the cabinet posts Haughey held he proved himself to be highly efficient.

But while he excelled in subordinate positions he was unable for the big one. On the three occasions he held this position his track-record has been one of rather dismal failure. In a sense he was very like Ludwig Erhard in Germany. Ludwig Erhard was probably one of the best economic ministers Germany ever had. He was responsible for what was known as the 'German Economic Miracle'. He was the envy of economic ministers all over Europe. Yet when he became chancellor after Adenauer he was a sorry failure. Like Haughey, he lacked the resolution, ruthlessness and guts required for top leadership.

In his private office Haughey has a plaque with the words: THINK BIG – but what use is thinking big if one cannot act big? Haughey lacks the broad insight, vision and determination of a great leader. He is very good at small-time, crossroads political foot-work but when it comes to the great all-embracing issues of statesmanship calling for breath of vision and international political skills he is simply lost. He is unable to distinguish between compromise and capitulation.

One of the first qualities needed by any leader of his people is nationalism or patriotism. In the case of Ireland that means a fundamental, unchangeable commitment to the concept of Ireland as a nation – and not just a state – a free thirty-two county nation with everything pertaining to that concept such as language, culture, identity, etc. This was the kind of nationality one found in De Gaulle, in Adenauer and even in Margaret Thatcher. Their patriotism was fundamental and unchangeable and it was this deep patriotism that motivated their entire political careers.

I felt deeply saddened a while ago when I read in an up-market British newspaper: 'Even his most ardent admirers would not claim that Mr Haughey is a man of principle.' I felt saddened because I knew in my heart that that statement contained a great deal of truth. For instance one could not make the same statement about John F. Kennedy in America or say De Valera or MacBride here in Ireland. Ideals and principles are by no means the dominating factors in Haughey's political life. Indeed, while only Haughey himself knows the answer, one cannot help feeling that the acquisition of votes, the maintenance of power are major driving forces behind him, and in the pursuance of such objectives most things even the abandonment of Fianna Fáil ideals play a role. It is worth noting his constant reference to a Unitary *State* – not a Unitary *Nation*. But he has not defined a unitary state. What does he mean? A unitary state within the British Commonwealth? That is quite feasable. But a unitary nation within the Commonwealth is simply a contradiction. Here again one should always take note of what Haughey does *not* say.

In a most intelligent and perceptive article in the *Irish Independent* Charles McGreevy, TD, had this to say about Haughey:

It is my opinion that he is at least not a good judge of people and their intentions. He is inclined to take people at face value and certainly if you plamás him he likes it very much. He loves to be liked.

This is a major weakness. It is one of the reasons why he surrounds himself with what can only be called clown princes. I've seen TDs playing up to him telling him downright lies for their own advancement and he believes them and seems to wallow in it and does not seem to see through it.

Indeed he seems to end up thinking very highly of that person. Told the truth that may be of value to him makes him hostile. People in the party have learned that the way to get on is to pay compliments to the 'Boss'.

This susceptibility to flattery is a most dangerous weakness in any leader. It seems to me that the British have sized up this weakness in Haughey and this may well account for the fact that he is now taking over from FitzGerald as the 'darling' of the British media. Sir Geoffrey Howe, foreign minister and Nicholas Fenn, the British ambassador in Dublin, have been the latest to praise him publicly. Is Thatcher far behind? He might well heed Parnell's words: 'When the British praise me I examine my conscience'.

Another important quality in any national leader is resolution. This may be variously described as guts, mettle, backbone, courage etc. In none of its different meanings or names could Haughey be said to excel. He hardly has the steel to stand up to his own shadow. He is weak, vacillating and irresolute when faced by someone British who stands up to him. He did not have the guts to stand up to Thatcher during the hunger-strikes. He seems totally mesmerised by her and becomes paralysed everytime she cracks the whip. The one occasion when, as a result of pressure from Fianna Fáil, he did stand up to her during the Malvinas/Falklands affair, she gave him such a trouncing that he never seems to have forgotten it and every time she faced him since he backed down like an errant schoolboy. She has won victory after victory over him. The Anglo-Irish Agreement and Extradition – she has won every round – and more recently she has slapped him in the face again over the Stalker affair, the Birmingham Six, the Prevention of Terrorism Act, the Gibraltar killings. All that has emerged from him is the occasional pip-squeek of a mild comment – but he *does* nothing.

It is in this field his great weakness lies. He seems to have a pathetic need for approval, especially British approval, and this deep-rooted need gives him the appearance of the mesmerised rabbit in the presence of a rattlesnake. The British know this and they have exploited it to the full in Anglo-Irish relations and won victory every time and in doing so made Fianna Fáil appear to the world as their partners in crime.

These two fundamental qualities were and are part and parcel of the make-up of great leaders but they are mostly absent from Haughey. He has the requisite ability to be a good subordinate but he seems unable for the mantle of leadership of a government.

When Haughey came to power in 1987 he found himself faced with a situation not unlike that of De Valera in 1932. De Valera had denounced the Treaty as Haughey had denounced the Anglo-Irish Agreement. But there comparison ended. De Valera unlike Haughey, did not go to America, eat humble pie and swallow his words. Instead he faced up to the British and began to dismantle the Treaty bit by bit. First he abolished the oath of allegiance to the British crown, then he witheld the annuities, then removed the governor general. Everywhere there was an outcry. The British pulled out every stop. They began a most terrible economic war against the Irish. They were unsparing in the use of all kinds of threats of further action. Here they were fully supported by Fine Gael. Abroad they enlisted the help of America, France, Spain and even the Vatican to pressurise De Valera. King Alphonso of Spain went out of his way to insult De Valera at international meetings. 'I have just seen that rascal De Valera. I cut him of course,' declared Alphonso. Cardinal Pacelli (later Pope Pius XII) brought every pressure possible to bear on the church in Ireland to ensure the re-election of Cosgrave and Fine Gael and the defeat of De Valera.

This economic war almost brought the country to its knees but De Valera held firm. When the British realised that the Irish leader was a man of steel they eventually capitulated. The treaty was forgotten and a new agreement was entered into which had an added bonus in that it gave us back the British occupied ports. De Valera wrote to a friend: 'If we win this fight England will never attempt to squeeze us in this way again!' This forecast however was not entirely correct. Forty years later when the British realised they had weak leaders like Lynch, Fitzgerald and Haughey they tried again to bring us to our knees with much more success.

Because we have no leader of the calibre of De Valera we may one day have to pay the price for all Haughey's capitulations and it is likely to be a terrible price. How many hundreds or indeed thousands of human lives will it cost? The British have tested us and found us wanting. They have taken our measure and they know that they can manipulate us almost any way they like. It is now but a short step to abandoning our neutrality and handing over our young men and women as cannon fodder – and we will not receive one iota in return. The Gestapo-type security forces will still hold sway in the six counties and we will be very lucky if they do not hold sway in the south too. The ideals of freedom that so many Irishmen and women gave their lives to defend are now almost in ruins. The Yeomen, the Black-and-Tans and the SAS are the victors to date.

Is there any hope? Certainly not from a government of Fine

Gael, PDs or Labour. They would have us, not on our knees, but flat out pleading with the British to spit on us, or indeed rushing to kiss the British prime minister on all four cheeks. Ireland is sick and broken as she has never been since the Famine. She is like a ship in a storm, rudderless and heading towards the rocks under the inept captaincy of milksops.

Will the youth of the country have to take more drastic means and occupy the GPO once again? Will they have to walk the lonely road to death as their fathers before them? I hope there is an easier way out.

But perhaps it is also true that the darkest hour comes before the dawn. There are signs among Ogra Fianna Fáil that the young people may resurrect the policies for which Fianna Fáil was founded and in doing so renew its idealism. There are strong indications that they are sick and tired of nods, winks, deals and strokes and tired of being kicked and spat upon by the British, sick and tired of incompetent leadership. Perhaps there may emerge from the wreckage of that great party some leader of ability who will bring us back to life, who will give us back our self-respect and who will weld us into a nation as De Gaulle, Adenauer, Gasperri welded their people into one, and as De Valera welded Ireland in the past when he stood up to the British in much more difficult times than the present. Freedom has an extraordinary way of surviving and in the end it usually wins the last battle.

In writing this sad distressful book I did not intend to hurt either Mr Haughey or any of his family. I leave that to others who seem to revel in it. Since I began political writing I have seen far too much hurt caused by the British occupation of Ireland and by their collaborators in the south. I have shared the wounds of hundreds of families whose sole breadwinner has been killed by the SAS or the RUC, often perhaps on a tip-off from the Irish security forces. I have shared the anguish of hundreds of women, old before their time, and their helpless children, whose husbands and fathers lie rotting in a British concentration camp. Again I have shared the trauma of relatives of so many young Irish men and women serving savage sentences in Irish jails for the 'crime' of wanting the British out of their country. These have been harrowing, if ennobling, experiences and I only regret that Charles Haughey did not share these experiences by visiting some of these families in their homes. But the circles Mr Haughey moves in are not those of the poor in the battered ghettos of the north or the corporation houses in the south; and that is all the greater pity, because I am sure if he did identify with them he would learn a great deal. He would I believe learn at first hand how many of these poor people identify with Terence MacSwiney's golden rule: 'not all the armies of all the empires of earth can crush the spirit of one true man – and that one man will prevail.'

I ended my book *The Statesman* with the words of Pearse: 'What if the dream comes true?' I was referring to Haughey's dream. Once again I apologise for being so far off the mark. The one thing Ireland does *not* want in the future is Haughey's dream. She deserves a better destiny.

MORE INTERESTING TITLES

BOBBY SANDS AND THE TRAGEDY OF NOTHERN IRELAND

John M. Feehan

Bobby Sands captured the imagination of the world when, despite predictions, he was elected a Member of Parliament to the British House of Commons while still on hunger-strike in the Northern Ireland concentration camp of Long Kesh.

– When he later died after sixty-six gruelling days of hunger he commanded more television, radio and newspaper coverage than the papal visits or royal weddings.

– What was the secret of this young man who set himself against the might of an empire and who became a microcosm of the whole Northern question and a moral catalyst for the Southern Irish conscience?

– In calm, restrained language John M. Feehan records the life of Bobby Sands with whom he had little sympathy at the beginning – though this was to change. At the same time he gives us an illuminating and crystal-clear account of the terrifying statelet of Northern Ireland today and of the fierce gurrilla warfare that is rapidly turning Northern Ireland into Britain's Vietnam.

THE SHOOTING OF MICHAEL COLLINS: MURDER OR ACCIDENT?

John M. Feehan

Was Michael Collins killed by an accident of war or was he ruthlessly murdered? Both of these possibilities are calmly and carefully examined by the author, who has rejected the traditional theory that he was killed as a result of ricochet rifle bullet and leans towards the possibility that he was shot by a Mauser pistol.

When the first and second editions of this book appeared they sold out instantly and caused a newspaper controversy which lasted many months.

In this third edition the author has rewritten large sections of the book incorporating new and rather startling information which came his way.

This new updated and rewritten edition is sure to arouse exceptional and absorbing interest in this baffling and bewildering mystery.